PREVAIL

A Handbook
for the
Overcomer

PREVAIL

A Handbook
for the
Overcomer

by
Kelley Varner

Destiny Image Publishers
P.O. Box 310
Shippensburg, PA 17257-0310

"We Publish the Prophets"

ISBN 0-938612-06-9

For Worldwide Distribution
Printed in the U.S.A.

Third Printing: 1986
Fourth Printing: 1991
Fifth Printing: 1994

AUTHOR'S NOTE

PREVAIL is ten years old. This handbook for the overcomer has found its way into every state and almost 40 nations. I am excited and grateful that this is its fourth printing. Much has happened in my life and in the Body of Christ since 1982. First of all, I am secure in my calling. I know that I am a scribe sent to the Church with a word of power and clarity, rooted in the emphasis of the glorious Person and the finished work of the Lord Jesus Christ. The Church has experienced the Feast of Passover and the Feast of Pentecost. Our Savior has washed away our sins in His own blood and has baptized us with the Holy Ghost and fire. Now we stand at the beginning of the decade that will usher in the Feast of Tabernacles, when God will dwell in the midst of His people and cause them to become a threshing instrument to harvest the nations of the earth. I know that He has chosen me to be a part of an apostolic ministry that is presently laying the foundation for this third Feast throughout the world. He is turning the hearts of the fathers to the children.

Secondly, I have written and published two other books, THE MORE EXCELLENT MINISTRY and THE PRIESTHOOD IS CHANGING. I will boldly declare that these three volumes, now a completed trilogy, will ground you in present truth and equip you for the days ahead. PREVAIL lays the foundation. THE MORE EXCELLENT MINISTRY reveals the present reality of the Most Holy Place. THE PRIESTHOOD IS CHANGING completes the set, unlocking the practical dynamics of moving from the Feast of Pentecost to the Feast of Tabernacles, from the Holy Place to the Most Holy Place, from adolescence to maturity. Underlying this change is the centrality and supremacy of the Lord Jesus Christ.

Thirdly, God has sovereignly opened the ear of His people. Men and women from every stream are abandoning once-cherished traditions as they are running after the Lord. These are days of unprecedented harvest. Stop being busy. Start becoming effective. Wisdom is the principal thing, and, with all your getting, get understanding. PREVAIL will thrust you into the pathway of His purpose.

The greatest blessing in your life is that you can still hear. He that hath an ear, let him hear...

Kelley Varner
September, 1991

TABLE OF CONTENTS

Page

FOREWORD

"To him that OVERCOMETH will I grant to sit with me in my throne, even as I also OVERCAME, and am set down with my Father in his throne" (Rev. 3:21; compare 2:7,11,17,26; 3:5,12; 21:7).

The TABLE is the way to the THRONE (Rev. 3:20). There is set before you a feast of principles of the Kingdom of God which will teach you how to "OVERCOME." This Greek word "NIKAO" means "to subdue, conquer, overcome, PREVAIL, get the victory." Webster defines "PREVAIL" to mean "to gain ascendancy through strength or superiority; triumph; to be or become effective." Herein are KEYS to effective Christianity.

Tens of thousands are being filled with the Holy Ghost. The Feast of Pentecost is becoming an experiential reality to hungry hearts everywhere. God is filling the earth with raw recruits for His army. Men and women from all walks of life are turning from the deadness of old order as the new age shines from Christ within.

This is not a day to confer with flesh and blood. God does not need the empty logic of man's reason to bring about this move of His Spirit. The Lord Jesus is building His Church! The people that He is designing to be a habitation of God through the Spirit are each resting on the solid foundation of His Word.

There are certain basic principles of the Kingdom of God that must be part of the believer's frame of mind. We must learn to think like God. We must begin to rule with Christ in this life. Too many Christians are weak and defeated. Their theology has miserably lowered their mentality into a world that revolves around self-comforts. May the dynamite of God's Spirit blow us all out of these "comfort zones" into a walk with God that is Christ-centered and not man-centered.

JESUS IS PRIEST AND KING. The Lord Jesus is a PRIEST Who is ever merciful and compassionate. He WILL and DOES meet the needs of man, but He is also the KING Who demands your obedience to His sovereign will. Is He your Ruler and Governor?

SALVATION IS PROGRESSIVE. The new birth is the beginning of our salvation. We have *been* saved, we are *being* saved, and we shall *be* saved. To grow is to change. The overcomer knows the BALANCE of the truth.

PRESSING THROUGH TRIBULATION. God keeps His people during the hour of trial. Too many misunderstand the dealings of God and have been taught to think that anything in the negative realm is of the devil. What does the Bible say about this? *BALANCE* is needed as we search the Scriptures for the answer.

Have you received the Baptism of the Holy Spirit and now find yourself restless and searching for more? Has the thrill worn off? Is the party over? Have the dealings of a loving Father torn up your spiritual playpen? If so, then YOU need to read this book!

Kelley Varner

These messages were preached in Wilmington, N.C. in the spring of 1981. They are available on three cassette tapes (VR414, VR415, and VR416). Write to:
Kelley Varner
Praise Tabernacle
P.O. Box 785
Richlands, NC 28574-0785
(919) 324-5026

I
JESUS IS PRIEST AND KING

God is a God of principle. He does not do anything by chance. Christians are not lucky. I believe that what happens in my life and yours is a result of the use or abuse of principles that we find in the Word of God. We will reap what we sow.

> *"Do not be deceived and deluded and misled; God will not allow Himself to be sneered at—scorned, disdained or mocked [by mere pretensions or professions, or His precepts being set aside].—He inevitably deludes himself who attempts to delude God. For whatever a man sows, that and that only is what he will reap" (Gal. 6:7 in the Amplified Bible).*

Would you like to see a "Bible result" in your church and city? I promise you upon the authority of God's Word that if you will put a Bible principle into motion, you will get a Bible result! I have proved it so. I encourage you to look with me to the Word of God.

God's people have never been so hungry for the reality of Him as they are right now. There is a Divine restlessness that has settled over the body of Christ. Pentecost is not enough. Speaking in tongues is not enough. Even the miraculous gifts and manifestations of the Spirit are not enough! We long for HIM!

"This is the Lord's doing; it is marvellous in our eyes. This is the day which the Lord hath made; we will rejoice and be glad in it" (Psa. 118:23-24).

Man did not make this new day, and man can't do anything about what God is doing in this hour. The Amplified Bible says, "This is the day which the Lord has brought about," and Moffatt adds, "This is a day we owe to the Eternal!" Like Mary of old, this visitation shall be accomplished without the help of man (Lk. 1:34). I know that God is again searching the earth for a VIRGIN, a habitation of PURITY. The Church has received the holy seed of the indwelling Christ. All that God IS is contained in that seed. ALL that the King IS and all that the King DOES dwells in you. Only God can plant it, and only God can make it grow (Gal 4:19).

"But our God is in the heavens: He hath done whatsoever he hath pleased ... And hath raised us up together, and made us sit together in heavenly places in Christ Jesus ... For it is God which worketh in you both to will and to do of His good pleasure" (Psa. 115:3; Eph. 2:6; Phil. 2:13).

The earth is the Lord's (Psa. 24:1). God has everything in the palm of His Almighty hand. He is sovereign. Jesus is King! Jesus is Lord! He knows everything that is happening, not only in the world system, but in your life and mine. This is the day that He has made. I want to be part of that day. Too long we have spent our time, talent, and treasure for that which satisfies not. (Isa. 55:2) Let us turn from the futility of religion and the never-ending pursuit of carnal ambition. The sweat of the first Adam has produced one man-made monument after another, and now the dust of the earth has covered their beauty.

We must give ourselves unto the *Word* of God, which is the *will* of God. We must begin to understand what God is doing in this hour, and do it with Him. Then we will find the joy of being an overcoming Christian. God has given us love letters, the Scriptures, that we might know the principles of His Mind. Practicing these precepts will result in a life of fulfillment instead of frustration.

WISDOM CRIETH WITHOUT

The book of Revelation pictures the Lord Jesus standing OUTSIDE the majority of the church world! Regardless of the label on the door, He stands outside most local churches and that which is labeled "Christian." What an indictment!

> *"Behold, I stand at the door, and knock: if any man hear my voice, and open the door, I will come in to him, and will sup with him, and he with me ... He that hath an ear, let him hear with the Spirit saith unto the churches" (Rev. 3:20,22).*

That verse was not written to the sinner. That verse was written to the church ... the CHURCH! The Lord desires to come into your church and send a mighty move of His Holy Spirit into every one of your lives. He wants to invade your homes and your jobs with the power of His Presence. God wants to resurrect us from our spiritual deadness and bring about a move of the Holy Ghost. He will still do it! He will do it when we:

> *"humble (ourselves), pray, seek, crave and require of necessity (His) face, and turn from (our) wicked ways; then will (He) hear from Heaven, forgive (our) sin, and heal (our) land" (2 Chron. 7:14 in the Amplified Bible).*

God will heal our land! He will heal our cities. He will heal our homes. He will heal our lives. But we must let

Him in. We must open to Him. Wisdom is crying without. Wisdom is a Person and that Person is Jesus (1 Cor. 1:30; Pr. 8:1-36; Jas. 3:17). Jesus, the Wisdom of God, is knocking on the heart's door of the Church with his HAND. The five-fold ministry of Eph. 4:11 is made up of apostles, prophets, evangelists, pastors, and teachers. He Who is the Bread of Life (Jn. 6:48) divided HIMSELF into five loaves when He ascended up on high. These ministries are the gift of Jesus to the Church. With one voice they are crying without:

> *"Wisdom crieth without; She uttereth her voice in the streets: She crieth in the chief place of concourse, In the openings of the gates: In the city she uttereth her words, saying, How long, ye simple ones, will ye love simplicity? And the scorners delight in their scorning, And fools hate knowledge? Turn you at my reproof: Behold, I will pour out my Spirit unto you, I will make known my words unto you" (Prov. 1:20-23).*

Wisdom stands on the outside of the church world. Another stance is mentioned in 1 Cor. 12:8-10. We speak specifically of the word of wisdom. THE word of wisdom is THE answer for a specific problem or situation. If you need an answer, you are saying you need the wisdom of God. Jesus is standing outside the organized church world with the answers. He is standing outside the educational and political and religious systems and He has all the answers. Young people sing a song: "Jesus is the answer for the world today." There is a present ministry crying with present truth (2 Pet. 1:12). Wisdom crieth without!

And WHERE is wisdom crying? In the streets. She cries in the chief place of concourse. In the opening of the gates. Let me apply this in a personal way: wisdom is crying at the gates of your eyes and ears. May your eye begin to see what the Bible says and your ear hear what

saith the Word of God to the churches. Note that she
uttereth her voice in the CITY. The first thing Jesus
called the Church was a CITY (Matt. 5:14; compare Gal.
4:26; Heb. 11:10; 12:22-23; Rev. 21:9-11). Again we see
that this whole passage in Prov. 1 deals with God's
people, the Church. Then verse 22 asks a question: How
long will the simple ones love simplicity? These simple
ones are also classified as scorners and as fools. The
word "SIMPLE" is an interesting word.

The Hebrew root word for "SIMPLE" is "PATHAH."
It is #6601 in Strong's Concordance and is rendered as
"to open, to be roomy, to be simple; allure, deceive,
enlarge, entice, flatter, persuade, silly one." The
Theological Wordbook of the Old Testament adds that
the verb "might relate to the IMMATURE or simple one
who is open to all kinds of enticement, not having
developed a discriminating judgment as to what is right
or wrong ... generally describes the NAIVE (not
deranged) in Proverbs who must be well taught, since an
IMMATURE person believes anything (Prov. 4:15)."
That describes many Christians today who have no
desire to grow up in God. They will strain at a gnat and
swallow a camel. They will believe (and preach) just
about anything! Wilson, in his O. T. Word Studies, also
says that this word means "simple, foolish, easily
enticed and seduced, credulous, inexperienced." For
further study see Psalms 19:7; 116:6; 119:130; Proverbs
1:4,32; 7:7; 8:5; 9:4,13,16; 14:15,18; 19:25; 21:11; 22:3;
27:12; and Ezekiel 45:20.

Thus to be simple is to be IMMATURE or
CHILDISH. There are too many Christians who want to
remain in the Outer Court of God's purpose. There is
little or no responsibility in that realm. Like Esau of old,
many want the BLESSING without the accompanying
RESPONSIBILITY of the BIRTHRIGHT. They love
the benefits, but they "DESPISE" the underlying
responsibilities (Gen. 25:34; Matt. 6:24). Note the
following:

OUTER COURT	HOLY PLACE	HOLY OF HOLIES
Little children	Young men	Fathers (1 Jn. 2:12-14)
Jesus the Babe	Jesus the Youth	Jesus the MAN (Lk. 1-3)
Passover	Pentecost	Tabernacles (Deut. 16:16)
Born of the Spirit	Developed	Matured (Eph. 4:13)
Out of Egypt	Through the wilderness	Into the land
Common salvation	Great salvation	Eternal salvation
30-fold	60-fold	100-fold (Matt. 13:23)
Workers	Warriors	Worshippers
Thanksgiving	Praise	Worship
Jesus (Saviour)	Christ (Anointed One)	The Lord
Way	Truth	Life (Jn. 14:6)
Faith	Hope	Love (1 Cor. 13:13)

There is more to this thing than just being born again. We must "grow up into Him in all things." (Eph. 4:15) This brings us to Prov. 1:23 and the challenge: "Turn you at my reproof!" God reproves us with the Word (2 Tim. 3:16). Listen to Wuest's translation from the Greek:

"Every scripture is God-breathed, and is profitable for teaching, for conviction, for improvement, for training with respect to righteousness."

The Amplified Bible says, "for REPROOF and conviction of sin." God wants us to turn or REPENT (change our MIND) at His Word! He is talking to the Church! This is the cry of the ministers of His wisdom. And then the writer reveals the PURPOSE of Pentecost. "Behold, I will pour out my Spirit unto you, I will make known my words unto you." How many of you have heard somebody quote Joel 2:28 or Acts 2:17?

"And it shall come to pass in the last days, saith God, I will pour out of my Spirit upon all flesh: and your sons and your daughters shall prophesy, and your young men shall see visions, and your old men shall dream dreams" (Acts 2:17).

He didn't say, "upon certain groups, or certain ministries, or certain nations, or certain doctrinal

persuasions . . . " He said, "ALL FLESH
years ago and it is still coming to pass! G
pour out His Spirit upon all flesh. What ..
it? What will we do with this new wine?

OPEN THE BOOK AND LOOSE
THE SEALS THEREOF

God has poured out His Spirit for the purpose of
opening the book. Jesus taught us that:

> *"The Comforter, which is the Holy Ghost, whom the
> Father will send in my name, he shall TEACH you
> all things, and bring all things to your remem-
> brance, whatsoever I have said unto you . . . when
> he, the Spirit of TRUTH, is come, he will guide you
> into ALL TRUTH: for he shall not speak of himself;
> but whatsoever he shall hear, that shall he speak:
> and he will shew you things to come" (Jn. 14:26;
> 10:13).*

May I make it simple? God wants to open His Word!
The Book has been closed. But God in His timing
planned to open the Book in this century. Hallelujah!
Daniel was instructed to:

> *"Shut up the words, and SEAL the book, even to
> the time of the end: many shall run to and fro, and
> knowledge shall be increased . . . the words are
> closed up and SEALED till the time of the end.
> Many shall be purified, and made white, and tried;
> but the wicked shall do wickedly: and none of the
> wicked shall understand; but the wise shall under-
> stand" (Dan. 12:4,9-10).*

So we see two kinds of people: the WISE and the
WICKED. Those who turn at the reproof of His Word

and those who scorn His principles. But one has PREVAILED to open the Book (Rev. 5:5)! This is the Day that God has chosen to unlock the secrets of His heart! We are the people upon whom the end of the age has come (1 Cor. 10:11). When the brethren speak of an end-time message, they are declaring that the END of this age is upon us and a new age is dawning. Perhaps we should be preaching the "beginning-time" message! The Sun of Righteousness has arisen. A new Day is upon us and we are glad!

Is the Book open or closed to you? Do you have a blinded mind or an open face (2 Cor. 3:14-18)? Has your heart turned to the Lord? God wants to pour out His Spirit upon your life that He might unlock the Word to you. Why? Because in this Bible are practical principles which apply to every area of your Christian walk. God does not want you sad and defeated. He does not want you frustrated or miserable. I know that God wants you to be strong, and vibrant, and healthy. Do you know that the JOY of the Holy Ghost is your STRENGTH (Neh. 8:10)? The only thing that will bring deliverance to the groaning creation and an apathetic church world is an outpouring—a deluge—of God's Spirit that will produce a "Bible revival" and a restoring of the principles of the Word of God to the minds and hearts of men. I am not talking of the reliving of the glory of a former day, but I am declaring the need of the pouring out of the Holy Ghost upon your life so that He can open the Scriptures to you that you might become aware of the present move of God in the earth.

God loves you. And He has given you more than a promise. He has given you the contract of His Kingdom. A covenant and an agreement signed in the blood of the Lamb (Jn. 1:29)! JESUS DIED AND LEFT YOU SOMETHING! The New Covenant is the last will and testament of the Lord Jesus. The writer to the Hebrews said that:

"[Christ, the Messiah] is therefore the Negotiator and Mediator of an [entirely] new agreement (testament, covenant), so that those who are called and offered it, may receive the fulfillment of the promised everlasting inheritance, since a death has taken place which rescues and delivers and redeems them from the transgressions committed under the [old], first agreement. For where there is a [last] will and testament involved, the death of the one who made it must be established. For a will and testament is valid and takes effect only at death, since it has no force or legal power as long as the one who made it is alive . . . He has once for all at the consummation and close of the ages appeared to put away and abolish sin by His sacrifice [of Himself]?" (Heb. 9:15-17,26b in the Amplified Bible).*

Jesus is the Testator of the New Covenant. His death put the New Testament into effect! And He has risen from the dead to become the Executor of His own will! Pulsing inside me is a sense of the need for God's people to know WHO they are and WHAT they have in Christ. Beloved, you are rich! You are blessed! You were blessed before you were born. You have been blessed with all spiritual blessings in heavenly places in Christ Jesus (Eph. 1:3), and you must perceive the riches of the glory of His inheritance in the saints (Eph. 1:18). I speak of the breadth, the length, the depth, and the height of Christ in you, the hope of glory (Eph. 3:18; Col. 1:27). But we will be blind and deaf and dumb to the vast Divine potential in the life of every believer as long as we allow MEN to tell us that we cannot be partakers of the Divine nature. And what is the KEY to becoming like Him?

"According as HIS DIVINE POWER hath given unto us all things that pertain unto life and GODLINESS, through the knowledge of him that hath called us to glory and virtue: whereby are given

unto us exceeding great and precious PROMISES: that by these ye might be partakers of the DIVINE NATURE, having escaped the corruption that is in the world through lust" (2 Pet. 1:3-4).

What is His Divine power? The Holy Ghost (Acts 1:8)! And the Spirit of God is being shed abroad to reveal the Scriptures, for in the Scriptures are the great and precious promises of our being conformed to the image of Jesus Christ. Paul also knew this, for he said that:

> "... we have received, not the spirit of the world, but the Spirit which is of God, that we might KNOW the things that are freely given to us of God" (1 Cor. 2:12).

There has been only one thing that will spoil and hinder your heritage. One thing that will keep your rightful possessions beyond your grasp or rip it from your hand if you ever begin to take hold of the things of God. The Lord Jesus tells us the answer in Mk. 7:13 when He said that MEN were making:

> "... the word of God of none effect through (their) TRADITION."

> "Thus you are nullifying and making void and of no effect [the authority of] the Word of God through your tradition" (Amplified Bible).

> "... so making the Word of God invalid" (Phillips).

> "... in order to protect your man-made tradition" (The Living Bible).

The only thing that can rob the Word of God of its power in your life is MAN-MADE TRADITION! Man's ideas, man's opinions, man's philosophies. Now you

know why the Pharisees are enraged at the thought of
YOU being filled with the Holy Ghost. They know all too
well that the Spirit will open the Word to you, and that
Word is setting fire to their deadly teachings. Jesus did
not come to bring life to the old order. He abolished it
(Col. 2:14).
Wisdom is crying without. The Spirit has been out-
poured and the Book is open. Jesus wants in. God will
change your life, your home, and your church in a way
that will amaze you. Let Him do exceeding abundantly
above all you can ask or think (Eph. 3:20). Forsake the
traditions of men and embrace a new day!

HOW TO BE HAPPY

I have entitled these three messages "Three Basic
Principles for the Overcomer." They are basic principles
of the Kingdom of God. They are foundational principles
for your happiness. I could go out on a limb and say that
they are requirements for your spiritual sanity. I might
have named this series simply as "How to be Happy."
So many Christians are not happy. There is no joy or
strength in their vessel. Their testimony has no "ring"
to it. Until the Church gets right, what can we offer the
world? If we proclaim the Gospel to the world with the
same countenance that the world already wears, what
good is it? We must speak a living word to a crippled
humanity that says "Such as I have give I thee: In the
name of Jesus Christ of Nazareth rise up and walk!" Let
us come to the groaning creation and say, "I have found
a better way of living. It is righteousness, and peace, and
joy in the Holy Ghost. I am serving the King. His name
is Jesus. He is Lord of my life. Come and see." That is
what the world needs to hear. But the majority of the
people of God are not happy.
Why? Because they are feeding upon a message that is
MAN-CENTERED and not GOD-CENTERED. They

only know Jesus in one dimension. There are many
facets to the wonders of His Person. Learn this basic
principle: JESUS IS A PRIEST AND A KING. The
majority of the church world is only interested in His
being a Priest or the Merciful One who meets the needs
of man. The blessed emphasis of the Word of God is His
LORDSHIP! He is to be King and Ruler and Governor
over my life and yours. Surely He will meet your needs
but he will also demand your obedience!

Everywhere we turn today, we hear a man-centered
gospel. Greedy ministry appealing to greedy people. The
carnal mind craves comfort and loves money. The
program of God does not center in man but is of,
through, and to Him (Rom 11:36)! The natural mind is a
fighter and a taker. The Mind of Christ is a Lover and a
Giver. The carnal mind is centered in self-rule. The
spiritual mind is centered in God-rule. Jesus is a Priest.
Jesus is a King. We must learn about BOTH dimensions
of His ministry. We cannot project a loving Priest
without the firm discipline of His Kingdom. And we
cannot preach the Gospel of the Kingdom without the
mercy and compassion of His Priesthood. Before we
continue further with this first message, we must
understand some basic teaching about the Kingdom of
God.

WHAT IS THE KINGDOM OF GOD?

The Kingdom of God is the extension of God's rule or
dominion in the earth and the universe. It is the territory
or area over which a KING rules and reigns. It is the
King's Domain. Webster's Dictionary adds that a
"kingdom" is "an area or a sphere in which one holds a
preeminent position." He also notes that a "domain" is
"a territory over which dominion is exercised." Who is
the King? JESUS! The Lord Jesus Christ is the King of
the Kingdom. Simply stated, the Kingdom of God is

defined in Scripture as being "righteousness, and peace, and joy in the Holy Ghost" (Rom. 14:17). It is wherever Jesus of Nazareth is Lord and King. The Kingdom is also the purpose and will of God (Matt. 6:10). It is a THEOCRACY; that is, a government that is GOD-RULED. The Kingdom is a PRESENT REALITY. It is not for ANOTHER TIME (the future only) or for ANOTHER PEOPLE (the natural Jew only).

It is sad that the traditions of men have taken the Kingdom of God and given it to another time and another people. That is an escape from PRESENT reality and responsibility. God loves ALL the races of the earth, and the Kingdom of God is not just for the natural Jew. But Jesus is the VINE, and the branches of that Vine are men and women of ALL nations (Jn 15:1-5)! Let us understand that the CHURCH is:

1. *Abraham's Seed (Eph. 2:11-12; Gal. 3:1-29; 4:21-31)*
2. *Spiritual Israel (Gal. 6:16; Rom. 2:28-29; 9:6-8)*
3. *The Circumcision (Phil. 3:3)*
4. *The Holy Nation (Mt. 21:42-43; 1 Pet. 2:9-10)*
5. *The New Jerusalem (Jn. 4:19-24; Gal. 4:21-31; Heb. 12:22-24; Rev. 21)*

My Christian friend, the JEW is YOU! Don't allow your previous teachings to rob you of the present reality of the Kingdom in your life. The devil doesn't care what you believe, as long as it is in the FUTURE! To long for the "good old days" or the "sweet by-and-by" is one way that the carnal mind escapes the emptiness of the NOW. Do you have the courage and honesty to face the God of the NOW? He is a very PRESENT help in trouble (Psa. 46:1). And He is proclaiming some present truth that is applicable and relevant to this day. God is saying something and He is saying something NOW! The Kingdom of God is a present reality. NOW faith IS (Heb. 11:1). King Jesus noted this truth when He said:

"The kingdom of heaven IS likened unto a man which sowed good seed in his field" (Matt. 13:24).

"The kingdom of heaven IS like to a grain of mustard seed" (Matt. 13:31).

"The kingdom of heaven IS like unto leaven" (Matt. 13:33).

"The kingdom of heaven IS like unto treasure hid in a field" (Mt. 13:44).

"The kingdom of heaven IS like unto a merchant man, seeking goodly pearls" (Matt. 13:45).

"The kingdom of heaven IS like unto a net" (Matt. 13:46).

The Kingdom of God is the Kingdom of Heaven. The term "Kingdom of Heaven" reveals where it is from, and the term "Kingdom of God" tells us Who runs it! And the Kingdom of Heaven IS! Then Jesus added that "the kingdom of God is AT HAND" (Mk. 1:15). Wuest's translation says, "The Kingdom of God has drawn near and is imminent." Goodspeed says, "The reign of God is near." Beck adds, "God's Kingdom is here!" And Phillips boldly declares, "The Kingdom of God has arrived!" Has the Kingdom of God arrived in your life? In your home? In your church? In your ministry? If Jesus is LORD in those dimensions, the Kingdom has come.

The Kingdom of God is at hand. It is within your reach! It is within the grasp of your hand! A lifestyle of righteousness, and peace, and joy in the Holy Ghost. Would you like to take hold of that? Righteousness is right living. This kind of righteousness is not positional, but functional. Right living is a missing commodity in today's world, but God is still interested in it. He wants folks to be right and to live right. And the Holy Ghost put Rom. 14:17 in the proper order, too, for until men live right, they will have no peace. Peace flows out of righteousness and then joy flows out of peace. Somebody asks, "How can I know if I am in the Kingdom? How can I discern Kingdom ministry?" The answer is given by the King Himself:

"Wherefore by their FRUITS ye shall know them" *(Matt. 7:20).*

"By their fruits you will clearly recognize them" *(Wuest).*

"You will fully know them" (Amplified) "by what they do" (Beck).

Kingdom people and Kingdom ministry are recognized by what they PRODUCE. Where there is righteousness, and peace, and joy in the Holy Ghost, King Jesus is reigning in that life or ministry. Where there is unrighteousness, turmoil, or sorrow, sombody else is in control. The Kingdom of God is available to you. John the Baptist came preaching this (Matt. 3:2). Jesus preached it (Matt. 4:17). The twelve apostles of the Lamb proclaimed the Gospel of the Kingdom (Matt. 10:1-8), as did the seventy also (Lk. 10:1-9). The ministries of the book of Acts declared the present reality of the Lordship of Jesus (Acts 1:1-3; 8:5,12; 20:24-25). When somebody is interested in knowing what we preach, tell them, "Brother Varner preaches the Gospel of the Kingdom." When they ask what that means, show them Acts 28:23 and say, "The Gospel of the Kingdom is a Gospel that PERSUADES MEN CONCERNING JESUS!"

We must proclaim a Christ-centered and Christ-honoring mesage with JESUS as the Focus and the Center. Jesus Christ is Lord, and He desires to impart His righteousness, peace, and joy to your spirit, mind, and body. The Bible says in Lk. 17:20-21 that this Kingdom is WITHIN you. The margin may render that as AMONG you or IN YOUR MIDST. What does that mean? Wherever you find the lordship of Jesus Christ actively operating, THERE is the Kingdom! The bottom line to all this is that these benefits are YOURS and they are yours NOW! The mentality that says that this life is a wilderness and that one of these days after we die we shall find some happiness, is a way of thinking that is totally unaware of the Word of God. Receive Him NOW!

DELIVERED FROM THE POWER OF DARKNESS

Jesus is Priest and King. Most Christians only relate to Him as the One Who is faithful to meet their needs (with physical needs the priority). Let me show you a verse that will help explain this principle:

"Giving thanks to the Father, Who has qualified and made us fit to share the portion which is the inheritance of the saints (God's holy people) in the Light. [The Father] has delivered and drawn us to Himself out of the control and the dominion of darkness and has transferred us into the kingdom of the Son of His love" (Col. 1:12-13 in the Amplified Bible).

Where is your inheritance? In Light. It is in the UNDERSTANDING of the Word of God (Psa. 119:105). We often hear someone say, "I got some light on that." They are declaring the reception of understanding. From the above Scripture we know there are TWO KING-DOMS: the Kingdom of God and the kingdom of darkness. Or the Kingdom of LIGHT and the kingdom of darkness. Satan's domain is marked by ignorance. He rules the unsaved, the unregenerated, the unconverted. Those who have rejected Jesus as Saviour boast of their "liberty," but the Bible says that:

"And you [He made alive] when you were dead [slain] by [your] trespasses and sins in which at one time you walked habitually. You were following the course and fashion of this world—were under the sway of the tendency of this present age—following the prince of the power of the air. (You were obedient to him and were UNDER HIS CONTROL,) the [demon] spirit that still constantly works in the sons of disobedience—the careless, the rebellious and the unbelieving, who go against the purposes of God. Among these we as well as you once lived and conducted ourselves in the passions of our flesh— our behaviour GOVERNED by our corrupt and sensual nature; obeying the impulses of the flesh and the thoughts of the mind—our cravings DICTATED by our senses and our dark imaginings. We were then by nature children of [God's] wrath and heirs of [His] indignation, like the rest of mankind" (Eph. 2:1-3 in the Amplified Bible).

An unsaved man is under the dominion of the devil. That was true of you and me, whether Jesus rescued us from the gutter or the church pew! As for me, I was a church-going hypocrite, and God saved me from the pew. I went to church all my life and the lord of darkness was my captain. My unregenerated mind was blind to the things of the Spirit of God. The natural man cannot know or understand the things of God. They are foolishness to him (1 Cor. 2:9-14). I had no desire for God, no desire for the Word of God, no desire for the Scriptures, no desire for prayer and no desire to let Jesus be the Lord of my life. Why? I was lost!

I was baptized in water when I was nine years old, but I came up a wet sinner. It didn't "take" that time. But when I was seventeen it did! God began to draw me to Himself and I got saved in the spring of 1966. I got baptized in water in the little church I grew up in. I'll never forget it. I wore a junior choir robe that was too

small for my six-foot frame, and a pair of tennis shoes. I
sang about God's "Amazing Grace" that morning, and
somebody asked, "What got into him?" Jesus Christ got
into me! Praise His Name! I once was BLIND, but now I
see! Peter said that you and I should:

"... *shew forth the praises of him who hath called
you out of DARKNESS into his marvelous
LIGHT" (1 Pet. 2:9).*

Isn't it marvelous to be a Christian? We have been
brought out of darkness and ignorance that we might be
transferred into the Kingdom of God. It is marvelous to
be saved. And what is in this light? Our inheritance (Col.
1:12)! No longer does the evil one have dominion over our
lives. Jesus has stripped him of his power and authority
(Col. 2:15; Heb. 2:14; 1 Jn. 3:8).

To this point we have been explaining the ministry of
Jesus as PRIEST. He is the Merciful and Compassion-
ate One who has saved us and brought us into His
domain. This is wonderful, but this is only the
BEGINNING. In His priestly ministry, Jesus comes to
you and reveals the love of God. He IS the Mercy of God,
the Forgiveness of God, the Blessings of God, the
Benefits of God, the Grace of God. How sad that most
Christians never progress beyond the understanding of
Who He is and why He was sent from the Father. Their
one spiritual ambition is to die and "go to be with the
Lord." But WHY were we saved? WHY were we brought
out of the kingdom of darkness into the Kingdom of
Light? To PARTAKE of something! To PARTAKE of
our INHERITANCE and to walk in what He died for!
God has brought us OUT that He might bring us IN
(Deut. 6:23). We have been PURCHASED and we have
been PURPOSED! There was a Divine intention that
brought about our redemption and it is serious. If we
miss the purpose to our purchase, what good is the
purchase? You BUY a car with the intent of driving that

car. Jesus the PRIEST has purchased us. Jesus the KING is purposing us. Let us not miss the fullness of God's moving in our lives by relating to Jesus in just one dimension.

Jesus is a Priest. Let me demonstrate this principle further with a passage of Scripture from the Song of Solomon. It will help us to see that some only want the Lord for what they can receive of Him.

"Because of the savour of thy good ointments thy name is as ointment poured forth, therefore to the virgins love thee" (Cant. 1:3).

The meaning of the word "VIRGINS" means "the hidden ones" (Psa. 83:3; 27:5; 31:20). This corresponds to the "simple ones" of Prov. 1:20-23. These people are innocent, young, veiled, and naive. Some can only relate to Jesus as Priest. They love Him because of His anointing and the power that is in His Name. The primary meaning of that word for "virgin" speaks of a young girl who was still hidden away in private, naive, and not knowing what was going on. One who is IMMATURE. People in this dimension are often over-balanced. These love the promise more than the God of the promise and wallow in a carnal and man-centered mentality that overemphasizes the blessed truth that Jesus has come to meet the NEEDS of man (Phil. 4:19).

Do you want to be an overcomer? Then learn that Jesus is Priest AND King. We have to move beyond the awareness that He is One who gives to others. He is also the One who said, "It is more blessed to give than to receive" (Acts 20:35). There is a prevailing attitude across the church world. There has been a projection of the Gospel to the multitudes that appeals to the flesh. This is how it comes across: "God loves you, and God wants to meet your needs." That is tremendously true! But if that is our EMPHASIS, if that is where we STOP, if that is the ONLY THING that we tell God's people,

then we are in trouble! If we pastors make that priestly
truth our priority, we will produce people who are
IMMATURE and SELFISH. We will build a church full
of takers and not givers. Then the people will become
upset with God every time He doesn't come running
when they quote their favorite "faith" Scriptures. A
warped presentation of truth will produce a warped
motive in the saints.

Do you understand what I am saying? God WILL and
DOES meet our needs. But we must be balanced. He has
delivered us from the powers of darkness, but a message
of death to self that others might live will send a
spiritual shudder through the minds of those who only
know Jesus as Priest. What has happened to the rugged
Pauline altar of knowing Him in the fellowship of His
sufferings? Immature ones who are easily miffed over
silly things have no place in the Kingdom of God. Those
who tell God in carnal impatience that He has failed to
meet their needs (more than likely the lusts of their flesh)
will be moved in this day of His shaking (Heb. 12:26-29).
Fear not to proclaim the Lordship of Jesus. It is
creation's only hope.

BEYOND THE BIRTH

If the message of the new birth (Jn. 3:1-8) is all we
preach, we will NOT move this generation! We must
move beyond the birth. We must preach basic salvation.
We must be evangelistic. But it will require "present
truth" (2 Pet. 1:12) to shake off the shackles of the
powers of darkness in this hour! Acts 2:38 is not enough.
We must move beyond the foundational principles and
begin to mature (Heb. 6:1-3). In Martin Luther's day,
justification by faith was a bombshell. But this is not
1525. At the turn of the century, Acts 2:4 was a
bombshell. But this is not 1900. Thank God for every
wave of God's tide of restoration that has brought a

people to the edge of His fullness. We will learn to be overcomers in this day or we shall be swallowed up and overcome by the birth pangs of a new age. And we will overcome as did the Pattern Son (Rev. 3:21), by fully submitting to the will of the One who is within.

The new birth is just that: a birth. A baby has his whole life before him as he learns to explore the world about him. And for us to say that the baby believer has tasted the whole of the Christian experience in his birth is ridiculous. From conception to perfection (maturity) we are growing from faith to faith, from glory to glory, and from strength to strength (Rom. 1:17; 2 Cor. 3:18; Psa. 84:7). The new birth is the beginning of your salvation. Your conversion is but the beginning of that which God is doing in your life. Salvation is a complete deliverance that God has in mind for your spirit, soul, and body.

So many today tie a knot in the rope and cry, "Hurry up, Lord! Come on, Lord Jesus, rescue me out of this mess!" They have a frame of mind that thinks "Just as long as I am born again . . . just as long as God is meeting my needs . . . I'm all right." This is an attitude of immaturity and selfishness. This is why there are few overcomers in the land. It is evident that they only know Jesus as Priest and not as King.

Why did the virgins in Song of Solomon 1:3 love Him? Why did the hidden ones love Him? I know that it is because they are also the VEILED ones. Their minds are blinded to His Lordship (2 Cor. 3:14-18). They love Jesus because of His anointing and because of His Name. But we must STAND in the Name while we speak in the Name. God is not interested in formulas, but whether we have identified with His NATURE and AUTHORITY in the Covenant relationship of wedded love. Immature love (the love that relates to Him only as Priest) is soulish and self-centered. It is based upon the outer or surface principles of the Lord's Name. The "virgins" are primarily occupied with what He DOES and not Who He

IS. While all the areas listed below are vital and foundational to this walk and ministry, they are just that: the BASIC principles and the foundation upon which we build (Heb. 5:11-6:3).

1. *Repentance and baptism in His Name. (Lk. 24:47; Acts 2:38)*
2. *Signs and wonders in His Name. (Mk. 16:17; Acts 4:30)*
3. *Casting out devils in His Name. (Mk. 16:17; Lk. 10:17-19)*
4. *Healing the sick in His Name. (Js. 5:14; Acts 3:6,16; 4:30)*
5. *Speak with new tongues in His Name. (Mk. 16:17; Acts 2:4)*
6. *Preaching and teaching in His Name. (Acts 4:7,17-18; 5:28,40)*
7. *Salvation in His Name. (Acts 2:21; 4:12; 16:31; Rom. 10:13)*
8. *Praise in His Name. (Rom. 15:9; Heb. 13:15; Eph. 5:20)*
9. *Gathering together in His Name. (Mt. 18:20)*
10. *Prayer in His Name. (Jn. 14:13-15; 16:24; 15:16)*

We love the power of His Name! It is wonderful to be able to say, "In Jesus' Name!" Praise His Name! But if that is the ONLY reason we love Him ... if we long for the power of His Name but have no time for HIM ... if we serve Him for what He DOES but never see Him as He IS, we will not be overcomers. Oh God, search our motives! He must, for we will continue to reproduce what we are.

We must see a demonstration of the power of God in our churches. Even in those places where the power of God is emphasized, we have only come to the edges of His ways. We have only touched the surface of the supernatural power and living energy that is in the Name of Jesus! Have you ever sensed your inadequacy?

Have you been content with your impotence or have you begun to pray for the release of His Omnipotence? We must see a ministry with signs following if the church is to be effective in this hour. This must be if we are to be true believers (Mk. 16:17). But if we go through our ministries and just tell folks "God loves you. Let Him meet your needs . . ." then they are going to receive a picture of a man-centered God. No! The plan of God centers in God! The world has heard a carnal projection of the Scriptures that God has done all of this for man. That is just not true! God has done all of this for Himself! A man-centered ministry is ever preaching what Jesus can do for you. Christ-centered ministry tells God's people that Jesus is LORD. Listen to these Scriptures:

> *"HE selected us out FOR HIMSELF in Him before the foundations of the universe were laid . . . in love having previously marked us out to be placed as adult sons through the intermediate agency of Jesus Christ FOR HIMSELF according to that which seemed good in HIS heart's desire" (Eph. 1:4-5 - Wuest's Expanded Translation).*

> *"Thou art worthy, O Lord, to receive glory and honour and power: for THOU has created all things, and FOR THY PLEASURE they are and were created" (Rev. 4:11).*

> *"For from Him and through Him and to Him are all things—For all things originate with Him and come from Him; all things live through Him, and all things CENTER IN . . . HIM" (Rom. 11:36 - Amp.).*

Did you know that man used to believe that the sun revolved around the earth? It was a shock to discover that the sun was the center! Jesus is the Light of the

world (Jn. 8:12) and the Sun of Righteousness (Mal. 4:2)
and the Day Star (2 Pet. 1:19). Too many Christians
want to be the center. Everything, including God, must
adjust to their little world. Have you noticed that little
children are like that? Children are selfish. Immature
Christians are selfish. Everything must revolve around
them. Their little world is their only concern. Beloved,
what God is doing won't fit on that postage-stamp-sized
self-centered frame of mind that is produced by
unbalanced preaching. Oh, for the time when children
grow up and understand that they are not the center of
things! Oh, for the day when my shepherd-heart shall
rejoice to see a people who understand that Jesus is
Priest AND King! JESUS IS THE CENTER!! Jesus is
King! Jesus is Lord!

*"He made known his WAYS unto Moses, His
ACTS unto the children of Israel" (Psa. 103:7).*

Israel knew His ACTS. They saw what God could DO.
Moses knew His WAYS. He understood the way that
God THOUGHT. But we who are privileged to be part of
this New Covenant can know His PERSON. We can
know Who He IS. It is not enough to know the WORKS
of God. It is not enough to know the WAYS of God. We
must run after HIM and the WONDERS of His Person!

AND HE SHALL GIVE THEE
THE DESIRES OF THINE HEART

There has been much taught to the Body of Christ in
the last fifteen years about the power of the SPOKEN
WORD. I have shared in communicating that awesome
and vital truth. Certain passages of Scripture have
become familiar to all of us (Mt. 12:34-37; Prov. 6:2;
Rom. 4:17; 10:6-10; Jas. 3:1-6). Indeed, the ministry of
the Kingdom of God operates on the principle of the

living Word (Mt. 21:18-23). But, like every other truth, this also demands balance. We are told, "You are what you SAY you are. You have what you SAY you have." And I know that you have heard this verse quoted more than once:

> *"Delight thyself also in the Lord; And he shall give thee the DESIRES of thine heart" (Psa. 37:5).*

The beastly carnal mind drools all over that verse. Come to Jesus and He will give you what you desire! No! That is NOT what that Scripture says. Look at it again. And put this verse with it:

> *"For it is GOD which worketh in you both to WILL and to DO of HIS good pleasure" (Phil. 2:13 in the KJV).*

> *"[Not in your own strength] for it is GOD Who is all the while effectually at work in you—energizing and creating in you the POWER and DESIRE—both to will and to work for HIS good pleasure and satisfaction and delight" (The Amplified Bible).*

> *"GOD is the One who is constantly putting forth His energy in you, both in the form of your being DESIROUS of and of your doing His good pleasure" (Wuest's Expanded Translation).*

> *"For it is GOD who energizeth within you both the DESIRING and the energizing" (Rotherham).*

> *"For it is GOD Himself whose power creates within you both the DESIRE and the power to execute His gracious will" (Weymouth).*

> *"Who makes you willing and gives you the energy to do what HE wants" (Beck).*

When David said in Psa. 37:4 that God would give us the DESIRES of our hearts, he did not mean that God would give us what WE want. He meant, rather, that the desires that are in us were given and placed there by the Lord. But those who know Jesus only as Priest, those who can only relate to a God Who meets their needs, those who are immature and carnal in thinking and action will ever butcher that verse to justify their own way of thinking.

PRESENTS OR PRESENCE?

Why are you serving God? Most folk serve Him because of His gifts. They love the gift more than the Giver. They love His presents more than they love His Presence. Do you want His presents or His Presence? Everybody will quickly say "I love the Lord!" But WHY do you love the Lord? Many will answer "I love Jesus because He saved me. He healed me. He baptized me with the Holy Ghost. He blessed me financially." That's not enough. If that is why you love Him, you desire gifts but not the Giver. If that is your frame of mind, you don't love the LORD (who is the KING); you love the PRIEST.

There is a "greenhouse" way of thinking in our country that has been preached, prophesied, and ministered to the Body of Christ. Don't peddle that to our bloodbrothers who are suffering and dying for the cause of Christ in other lands. Some have foolishly tried, but they can't hear you. They cannot relate to a message of those who say,"You will never have to suffer. You will never have to hurt. You will never have to sacrifice. Just come to Jesus, and everything will be all right. As long as you are born again, He will come any minute to rapture you out of all your troubles and pressures." Men and women who take the Kingdom of God seriously cannot receive those lies. Following Jesus Christ will cost you your life (Mt. 16:24-26; 19:21-22; Lk. 9:23; 14:26)!

I don't want to upset you, but there are so many who love God for one reason: what He has done for them. That IS a good reason. We all started there. Jesus is our Merciful Saviour. He is Priest. But if we STOP there, if we bog down and stagnate at that starting point, if we build doctrinal and sectarian walls around those foundational truths, we will cut off God's moving in our lives. Our people will be imprisoned and bound by our own unbelief. May God challenge the heart of every leader in the Body of Christ to take another look at his motive, his vision, and the kind of mind he is imparting to his hearers. I have counseled with too many frustrated pastors. They have reproduced their restless spirit in their people. They have stopped growing. Organizational limitations have bound their hands and they cannot embrace this new day (Luke 2:28). We must know Jesus as Priest AND King. We must instill that balance in the lives of the people we lead. We must teach them by example and precept to love His Presence more than His presents.

THE LAW OF LOVE IS GIVING

God's purpose is that we be just like Him. God is a Giver and God is LOVE (1 Jn. 4:8,16). The law of love is GIVING. We are to be conformed to His image, for the Scripture says that:

> "... God so LOVED the world that he GAVE his only begotten Son, that whosoever believeth in him should not perish, but have everlasting life... as my Father hath sent me, so send I you" (Jn 3:16; 20:21).

Those who know Jesus only as Priest are takers and

not givers. It is much more blessed to give than to
receive. I know that you love the Lord. I know that you
love the Bible. So do I. But can we pop a spiritual
thermometer in our mouths? Can we be honest enough to
re-evaluate our motives? Let us examine ourselves,
whether we be in the faith (2 Cor. 13:5).

God is pouring out His Spirit and opening up the Word
to challenge the Church to do something that the Church
does not want to do: grow up! We must grow up and
become like Him. And God is not a taker; He is a Giver. I
can gauge the spiritual atmosphere of a church by
counting how many "Georges" (one-dollar bills) there are
in the plates. Why don't we give God a raise? I am not
speaking about finances. I am speaking about
NATURE: His nature. The nature of love is self-
sacrificial. It gives without expecting anything in
return. Why do you give? Why do you serve Him? Why
do you love Him?

Jesus is a Priest. He loves you and He meets your
needs; but if our understanding of God ends there, we
will miss the purpose of His great salvation. The Bible
says that:

> "... the eyes of them both were opened, and they
> knew that they were naked; and they sewed fig
> leaves together, and made themselves APRONS ...
> unto Adam also and to his wife did the Lord God
> make coats of skins, and clothed them (Gen. 3:7,21).

Adam and Eve made themselves aprons. What did
these cover? Only the FRONT. The church world is *still*
making aprons! Some wear the man-made apron of fig
leaves apart from the blood atonement of Jesus. Others
wear the apron of knowing Him only as Priest but not as
King. Some are wearing a RELIGIOUS FRONT! If this
move of God turns us around, everyone is going to see
what we really are! I don't want to wear a mask. I don't
want to play church. I don't want to be part of a "loaves

and fishes" crowd that is following Jesus just to see something or to get something. I don't want to partake of that abominable thing called religion. I don't want it! Religion ministers death, and the creation is groaning for life! Let us minister LIFE, for:

> *"[It is He] Who has qualified us (making us to be fit and worthy and sufficient) as ministers and dispensers of a new covenant [of salvation through Christ], not [ministers] of the letter—that is, of legally written code—but of the SPIRIT; for the code [of the Law] kills, but the [Holy] Spirit makes alive" (2 Cor. 3:6 in the Amplified Bible).*

Jesus is Priest AND King. If He is Lord, then He can lay hold of my time, for it is really His time! He is King of my talent, which is actually His talent. Jesus rules my treasure, which is actually His treasure (1 Chron. 29:14). The King of the Kingdom can have these things any time He pleases. We are dead to sin and alive to God (Rom. 6:11). A dead man has no rights. A dead man does not argue. A dead man doesn't complain. A dead man is an overcomer!

Some of you need to enjoy this walk with King Jesus. If He invites you to supper, He will pick up the tab! That is HIS responsibility! Once I surrender my life to HIS LORDSHIP, He is responsible to take care of me. I don't serve Him for that reason, but it is good to know! We sing a chorus in our assembly that goes like this:

I WAS BORN TO BE THY DWELLING-PLACE,
A HOME FOR THE PRESENCE OF THE LORD,
SO LET MY LIFE NOW BE SEPARATED
UNTO THEE,
THAT I MAY BE WHAT I WAS BORN TO BE.

I have a message from the King. He knows that you love Him. He knows that He has brought you out of

darkness and into His marvelous light. Now Jesus wants
to mature you and bring you into a lifestyle of
dedication, consecration and service in His Kingdom.
The Lord knows we will never be overcomers until we
dispense this life of Jesus into others.

I have found a secret. I have discovered the key that
will unlock the door to a Spirit filled with His dominion. I
know what will strike fear in the heart of the enemy. We
must relate to Jesus as priest AND King! If we stop
with the priestly principle, we will come short of God's
best for our lives and ministries. The prophet Daniel saw
two kinds of people in the end of this age:

> *"And he shall speak great words against the Most*
> *High, and shall WEAR OUT the saints ... but the*
> *people that do KNOW their God shall be STRONG,*
> *and DO EXPLOITS" (Dan. 7:25; 11:32).*

Those who only serve God for His benefits are being
worn out. They flock unto anyone who will lay hands on
them to patch up the old man, especially in the physical
or financial realms. Their beggar's cup rattles from coast
to coast. Brother, throw away your tin cup! Sister, cast
off your beggar's garments! We are to be Israelites (Gen.
32:24-32). We are to be princes, the sons of a King! We
are to be those who have power with God and man:
prevailers and overcomers! Those who KNOW God as a
Priest AND King are walking in the strength and joy of
their Lord.

FROM WHENCE WE LOOK

Without a prophetic vision, God's people will perish
(Pr. 29:18). The higher you go, the farther you can see.
Let us arise from the dust of carnality and lusting after
what we can get from God. Where is your focus? Lift
your eyes to new horizons (Jn. 4:35). Look from the top

of the mountain (Song of Solomon 4:8). Did you know that:

> "... *our conversation is in heaven, from WHENCE we look" (Phil. 3:20).*

If we preach a man-centered vision that only emphasizes a God who meets the need of humanity, we will miss the God-centered vision that everything is of Him, through Him, and unto Him. He is Lord! He has risen from the dead and He is Lord! I weep for the many people that I have met in many places. People and even pastors from all over the country have written or called me, and so many are crying out in frustration and desperation for answers. I am reminded of the words of Joel the prophet:

> *"Multitudes, multitudes in the valley of DECISION: For the day of the Lord is near in the valley of decision" (Joel 3:14).*

That word "decision" could be rendered "DETERMI-NATION." God is making demands upon our lives. We must decide which way to go. We will determine to remain as we are, or we shall determine to move with God. There can be NO neutrality (Mt. 6:24; 12:30-33). We have misrepresented the Lord Jesus. Some are saying, "Try Jesus," as if He is some kind of free sample. And the world has looked on and has seen a people as miserable as they are. The creation will not be liberated by beggars. There is coming forth a glorious Church without spot or wrinkle (Eph. 5:25-27). Jesus cannot come again until such a people arises in the earth and overcomes as He overcame (Acts 3:19-21; Eph. 4:11-13; Js. 5:7; Psa. 110:1 with Heb. 10:12-13; Rev. 3:21)!

God is bringing us out of the immaturity of just knowing Him as Priest. He is bringing us into a realm where Jesus is LORD! That people will say as did the three Hebrew children:

"If it be so, our God whom we serve is able to deliver us from the burning fiery furnace . . . BUT IF NOT, be it known unto thee, O king, that we will not serve thy gods, nor worship the golden image which thou hast set up" (Dan. 3:17-18).

There is a realm of living and ministry that goes beyond the priestly function and spans the dimension where Jesus is Lord. Let us take a sincere look at our lives. Let us love God for Who He is and not what He has done or what we receive from Him. We must be trained and disciplined as sons if we are to become that overcoming people He has called us to be. God has always wanted a Kingdom of priests (Ex. 19:1-6). Priests and kings . . . just like Jesus. That is why we must learn to see Him and know Him in BOTH dimensions.

"Beside this you know what [a critical] hour this is, how it is high time now for you to wake up out of your sleep—ROUSE TO REALITY. For SALVA-TION (FINAL DELIVERANCE) is nearer to us now than when we FIRST believed . . . The night is far gone [and] the day is almost here. Let us then drop (fling away) the works and deeds of darkness and put on the [full] armor of light" (Rom. 13:11-12 in the Amplified Bible).

Hallelujah! Full salvation! Final deliverance! Arise and walk in the light of a new day. Cast off the works of ignorance. God is not a glorified Santa Claus or the manager of a heavenly supermarket where we can pick and choose at our leisure. He is:

" . . . a God of gods, and a Lord of kings . . . And he hath on his vesture and on his thigh a name written, KING OF KINGS, AND LORD OF LORDS" (Dan. 2:47; Rev. 19:16).

"For God is my KING of old, Working SALVA-
TION in the midst of the earth ... The Lord shall
reign for ever, even thy God, O Zion, unto all
generations" (Psa. 74:12; 146:10).

II
SALVATION IS PROGRESSIVE

There are certain basic principles for those who desire to be part of a redeemed society. First, we must understand that Jesus is both a Priest and a King. He is the One Who meets the needs of man but He is also the One Who demands the obedience of man. In this second message we will discover that salvation is both once-for-all and presently progressive in the Christian walk.

God wants a happy people. He wants a victorious people. So many claim that the joy of the Lord is in their heart, but they have yet to notify their face! Out of the abundance (overflow) of the heart the mouth will speak (Matt. 12:34). If there is joy and praise and thanksgiving and gladness in our hearts, then it surely must spill over into our countenance and everyday walk with the Lord.

In the previous message I shared with you some basic principles pertaining to the Kingdom of God. The Kingdom of God is not for another time or another people . . . it is for you NOW! It is at hand. The Kingdom of God, or the Kingdom of Heaven, is that dimension in which Jesus Christ is Lord. He is Ruler and Governor over our lives.

However, there are those who have no desire for His Lordship. They relate to Jesus as Priest, but not King. I know that is one reason why some Spirit-filled Christians are frustrated, nervous, apprehensive and miserable. Selfish believers only want the benefits, the gifts, and the grace of God without the accompanying responsibilities.

"For unto whomsoever much is given, of him shall be much required" (Lk. 12:48).

"Much will be expected" (Twentieth Century N.T.).

"Much will be demanded" (Williams).

Do you remember Esau of the Old Testament? The Bible says that God loved Jacob but hated Esau (Mal. 1:2-3; Rom. 9:13). Why? To find the answer we must recall the account of Gen. 25:27-34 where Esau sold his BIRTHRIGHT and the passage in Gen. 27:1-35 where Jacob swindled his brother out of the BLESSING. There was a difference between the birthright and the blessing.

James Freeman, in his Manners and Customs of the Bible, says, "Great respect was paid by the household to the first-born son. He had headship over his brothers; he succeeded to the father's official authority; he had a special claim to the father's benediction (blessing); in him was the progenitorship of the Messiah; the domestic priesthood belonged to him, according to some authorities, though this is denied by others. Under the Mosaic law he received a double portion of his father's goods."

To receive the birthright was to receive RESPONSIBILITY! Esau took two things from Jacob: the birthright and the blessing. Later, when God began to deal in his life, Esau still wanted the blessing, but he never wanted the birthright. With those rights came certain responsibilities. So it is with us who have been born of God's Spirit. The believer has his own written Bill of Rights! They are the many benefits and precious promises of the blood covenant of the New Testament. We have privileges as a child of God, but there are underlying responsibilities. Specifically, we must

GROW UP and mature in Christ, and the more we grow, the more we accept the challenge of being an overcoming Christian. God demands growth.

God hated Esau because he DESPISED his responsibilities as a son. The word for "DESPISED" in Gen. 25:34 is "bazah" (#959 in Strong's) and means "to disesteem, despise, disdain, condemn, scorn; vile person." The Theological Wordbook of the O. T. notes that this word "appears with its derivatives forty-three times in the O.T. The basic meaning of the root is 'to accord little worth to something.'" Wilson, in his Word Studies adds, "to slight, neglect, make little account of, to treat contemptuously or proudly; it is opposed to the act of esteeming, appreciating, or caring for." This, then, was the attitude of Esau toward his birthright. And God feels the same way toward those who love the benefits but continue to proudly despise the responsibility that accompanies those blessings.

The majority of the church world is selfish. The proof of that is the popular widespread "escapism" mentality that has become a sacred cow to so many. But we have yet to fulfill Jesus' Great Commission, for He said,

> *"All power is given unto me in heaven and in earth. Go ye therefore, and TEACH all nations, baptizing them in the name of the Father, and of the Son, and of the Holy Ghost: TEACHING them to observe all things whatsoever I have commanded you" (Mt. 28:18-20).*

There are two Greek words for "TEACH(ING)" in that passage, and there are two great principles revealed here that we must keep in balance in our lives, in our local churches, and in our ministries. Note these two words:

1. "TEACH all nations" - "MATHETEUO" (#3100 in Strong's) - "to become a pupil; to disciple, to enroll as a scholar."

   2. "TEACHING them"- "DIDASKO" (#1321 in
Strong's) - "to teach; to give instruction."

How big is your vision? The wind blows all over the
world, and those who have been born from above have a
world-wide vision (Jn. 3:8). The Lord told us to enroll the
nations and then teach them everything He commanded! To do that demands EVANGELISM and then THE
INSTRUCTION OF GOD concerning the overcoming
life. We are to reach the lost and then teach them all
things.
   Some churches are only interested in the first part of
that command. They don't want to teach the saints.
God's people are not being fed in those places. There is
no message of life that will make Christians grow up.
The basic truth of the born-again experience is preached
every Sunday to a house full of born-again people. The
result is a large church full of babies and starving
believers.
   On the other hand, some churches are only interested
in the second part of the Lord's marching orders. They
want the "deeper life." They don't want to be wise
(Prov. 11:30). There is no evangelistic vision. These kind
of folk want a constant diet of exotic spiritual food, but
nothing staple or basic. "Feed us the Word," is their cry.
"What is your latest revelation, Varner?" "Give us
something rich." But they are not the least bit
interested in seeing somebody saved. There hasn't been
anyone baptized in water or filled with the Holy Ghost in
some of those places for years, and then if it does
happen, they talk about it for another year! They, too,
are out of balance. If we are to be healthy in the Lord, we
must have a vision and a diet that is BALANCED! We
must fulfill BOTH aspects of the Great Commission! We
must see new lives born into the Kingdom, for any
church or group that does not reproduce itself will die.
We must also be able to instruct these new believers
from the realm of conception to the realm of perfection.

This is not an option. It is the mandate of the King Himself. And Jesus was interested in sinners. The woman at the well, Zacchaeus, blind Bartimaeus, Nicodemus, not to mention you and me! Yet He was also the Pattern and Example and the greatest Teacher that man ever heard!

We need BOTH these principles! This truth is beautifully revealed in the book of Ruth where Boaz, the Kinsman-Redeemer and a type of our Lord Jesus, said to the woman (the Church):

> *"Let thine EYES be on the FIELD that they do REAP, and go thou after them . . . AND when thou art athirst, go unto the vessels, and DRINK of that which the young men have drawn" (Ruth 2:9).*

Let your eyes be on the field. The field is the world (Matt. 13:38). Maintain a VISION for the lost! Be evangelistic. Reach out. Get a burden for the lost and the young people in your city! Don't be satisfied until your altars are filled with sinners, repenting and weeping their way through to an experience with God. Follow the reapers. Go thou after them!

But also drink and feed when you are thirsty and hungry. It is not enough for you to be evangelistic. You must know what it is to feed upon the Word of God and the Holy Ghost within. Learn what it is as a believer to mature and develop. Grow in the grace and knowledge of the Lord Jesus Christ.

Jesus commanded His followers to do two things. Make disciples of all nations. That is evangelism. But after folks accept Jesus as their Saviour, do something for them. Teach them. Not "some" of the things, not "a few" of the things; we are to teach them "ALL" things that He taught. What did Jesus teach?

THE PRINCIPLES OF THE DOCTRINE
OF CHRIST

"Concerning this we have much to say which is hard to explain, since you have become dull in your [spiritual] hearing and sluggish, even slothful [in achieving spiritual insight]. For even though by this time you ought to be teaching others, you actually need some one to teach you over again the very first principles of God's Word. You have come to need milk, not solid food. For every one who continues to feed on milk is obviously inexperienced and unskilled in the doctrine of righteousness, [that is, of conformity to the divine will in purpose, thought and action,] for he is a mere infant—not able to talk yet! But solid food is for full-grown men, for those whose senses and mental faculties are trained by practice to discriminate and distinguish between what is morally good and noble and what is evil and contrary either to divine or human law.

Therefore let us go on and get past the ELEMENTARY STAGE in the teachings and DOCTRINE OF CHRIST, the Messiah, advancing steadily toward the COMPLETENESS and PERFECTION that belongs to SPIRITUAL MATURITY. Let us not again be laying the FOUNDATION of repentance and abandonment of dead works [dead formalism], and of the faith [by which you turned] to God, with teachings about purifying, the laying on of hands, the resurrection from the dead, and eternal judgment and punishment. [These are all matters of which YOU SHOULD HAVE BEEN FULLY AWARE LONG, LONG AGO.] If indeed God permits we will [now] proceed [to advanced teaching]" (Heb. 5:11-14; 6:1-3 in the Amplified Bible).

This was written to Christians. It is time to get out of

our spiritual diapers and start giving out what we should already have learned a long time ago! Some have spent all their lives in church. It is time to grow up! If you preach the new birth Sunday after Sunday to a room full of Christians, your church will stagnate in the Spirit and die. All you will have is a "big barn" (Lk. 12:18). There is more to this walk than just being born again. That is the beginning of your experience with God. And we had better preach and practice that blessed truth! But these are first principles. These are the basics, the truths you learn in God's elementary school. The MILK of the Word. Desire it, that you may GROW thereby (1 Peter 2:2).

If we are to be perfected (matured) in Him, we must leave these basics. That does not mean that we STOP teaching or practicing these blessed truths, but we must lay this solid FOUNDATION and then build God a house upon that base. Lay the foundation! Lay it well (Matt. 7:24-27; Lk. 6:46-49)! God will not issue you a heavenly "building permit" (Heb. 6:3) until you do! The early Church built on the solid rock of the foundational teaching ministry of Jesus Christ:

1. REPENTANCE FROM DEAD WORKS. (Acts 2:38; 5:31; 3:19; 8:22; 17:30; 26:20; 13:24; 19:4; 20:21)

2. FAITH TOWARDS (UPON) GOD. (Acts 3:16; 6:5-8; 11:24; 13:8; 14:9,22-27; 15:9; 16:5; 20:21; 24:24; 26:18)

3. DOCTRINE OF BAPTISMS. (Acts 1:5; 2:38-41; 8:12-16,36-38; 11:16; 9:18; 10:46-48; 16:15,33; 18:8; 19:3-5; 22:16)

4. LAYING ON OF HANDS. (Acts 4:30; 5:12; 6:6; 8:17-19; 9:12,17,41; 11:21; 11:30; 13:3; 14:3; 19:6; 28:8)

5. ETERNAL JUDGMENT. (Acts 7:7; 8:33; 10:42; 13:46; 24:25; 1:15-26; 5:1-11; 13:6-12; 28:25-28)

6. RESURRECTION OF THE DEAD. (Acts 1:22; 2:31; 4:2,33; 17:18,32; 23:6-8; 2:24-32; 3:22-26; 13:22-23,30-37; 26:8; 7:37; 10:40; 17:31)

There are ministries in the land today that do not and will not teach the principles that Jesus taught and upon which the apostles built the Church (Eph. 2:20)! I am told by certain "scholars" that these truths are no longer applicable to the Christian experience. We are not to fulfill the Great Commission and teach what the Lord Jesus taught. And that is why we do not see the RESULTS that Jesus had! Do you have enough spiritual perception to see the truth of this verse?

"If the foundations be destroyed, what can the righteous do?" (Psa. 11:3).

"When the pillars are overthrown . . ." (Rotherham).

"For when the foundations are broken down . . ." (Harrison).

"The pillars of the State are falling: what can a just man do?" (Moffatt).

God is building a mansion for Himself (1 Chron. 29:1). He is creating a people who shall be the city and the habitation of God through the Spirit (Matt. 5:14; Rev. 21:9-10; Eph. 2:19-22). My heart is broken for the ignorance that enslaves the children of God. How can we become God's house without a solid foundation? Yet the scribes and the lawyers clamor for His coming. How can He come when those who have taken His Name will not even believe His Word concerning the basics of His Kingdom (Acts 3:19-21; Eph. 4:8-16; Heb. 10:12-13)? The uncertain sound of a mixture of His truth and our tradition has leavened the whole lump, for as yet He still has no certain dwelling place (1 Cor. 14:8; 5:6-8; Matt. 16:12; Isa. 66:1; 1 Cor. 4:11). The Lord Jesus still has no place to lay His Headship (Matt. 8:20). We do not want His MIND and will and purpose to spoil our eschatology. There is no room for HIM (Lk. 2:7). I tell you of a truth, God is not only going to "rock" the boat of man's theology; He is going to sink it!

In this day when "new carts" are so prevalent (1 Chron. 13:7), we must lay a solid foundation by removing all the dirt between us and the Rock. We must dig deep. After our foundation is tried (Isa. 28:16), God will give us His building permit, for He will only honor His own building code (Psa. 127:1)! God is building a house, and He has commissioned a team of ARCHITECTS to see to it that this house of the King is brought to completion. They are the ministries of Eph. 4:11 (compare 1 Cor. 3:10—"masterbuilder" is "archetekton" in the Greek). They have the authority of the King to carry out His Commission. The King has given nine different TOOLS (power tools at that!) to these architects (1 Cor. 12:8-10). How sad that so many who claim to be the King's subjects will tell us that these tools are outdated. Let it be declared throughout the land! Hear the proclamation of the King:

"ANY HOUSE BUILT IN THE NAME OF THE KING THAT IS NOT CONSTRUCTED ACCORDING TO HIS PLAN SHALL BE BURNED WITH FIRE!"
(Jer. 23:29; 1 Cor. 3:1-15; Heb. 12:26-29)

FOUNDATIONAL THINGS

Salvation is progressive. We must lay the foundation to our walk with the Lord and then begin to grow. The writer to the Hebrews mentioned "repentance from dead works, and of faith toward God" (Heb. 6:1). REPENTANCE and FAITH. These are the two basic elements of conversion. In this day of "easy believism," repentance is a "bad word." Many are saying, "Just believe!" Repentance is an old-fashioned word that has

gone out of style. But John the Baptist preached it
(Matt. 3:1-12) and JESUS preached it (Mk. 1:14-15)! On
the Day of Pentecost Peter preached repentance (Acts
2:38). I am going to identify with those who proclaim a
message that makes men change their way of thinking! I
will say more about repentance later.

Faith "toward" God is literally faith "upon" God.
Casting all your care upon Him (1 Pet. 5:7). Faith for
conversion. Faith for divine healing. Faith for the
infilling of the Holy Ghost. Faith for finances. This is
foundational faith. This is BASIC faith. Some of God's
people have finally started to elementary school.

Then he adds, "the doctrine of baptisms." That, too, is
milk. Note that this is BAPTISMS. Plural . . . more than
one. In the Outer Court of God's purpose there is an
experience of WATER BAPTISM in the Name of the
Lord by immersion. In the Holy Place dimension we will
experience THE HOLY GHOST BAPTISM. It's like
buying a pair of shoes: the TONGUES comes with it
(Acts 2:4; 8:18-21; 9:17 with 1 Cor. 14:18,39; Acts
10:44-46; 19:1-6)! And in the realm of the Most Holy
Place there is A BAPTISM OF FIRE. You should know
that . . . the doctrine of baptisms. Jesus taught this, but
because of tradition, we have gotten away from the
Word of God and what Jesus taught. Thank God that
many of His servants are waking up to reality!

Then Heb. 6:2 mentions "the laying on of hands." This
is a Biblical method of conferring Divine blessing. The
anointed hands become the channel, the vehicle, the
bridge by which something is transferred or transmitted
from one person to another. The three words that define
this basic ministry are IDENTIFICATION, IMPAR-
TATION, and CONFIRMATION. Some of the purposes
for the laying on of hands are:

1. For healing the sick *(Matt. 8:3,15; Mk. 6:5; 16:18;
Acts 5:12; 19:11).*

2. For blessing children *(Matt. 19:13; Mk. 10:16).*

3. For conferring the Holy Spirit *(Acts 8:18; 9:17; 19:6).*

4. For blessing, ordination, and prophetic impartation *(Gen. 49; Lk. 24:50; Acts 6:6; 9:17).*

NOTE: This latter ministry is in the O.T. AND the N.T.)

There are those who scoff at the thought of the healing power of the risen Lord of Calvary imparted through the laying on of hands, but they are those of whom Paul warned us:

> *"See to it that no one carries you off as spoil or makes you yourselves captive by his so-called philosophy and intellectualism and vain deceit (idle fancies and plain nonsense), following HUMAN TRADITION—men's ideas of the material [rather than the spiritual] world—just crude notions following the rudimentary and elemental teachings of the universe, and disregarding [the teachings of] Christ, the Messiah" (Col. 2:8 in the Amplified Bible).*

Through the blood Covenant of Jesus Christ, God has made a full provision for us and I refuse to keep quiet about it! May God be merciful to those who are telling God's people that they cannot partake of the blessings of Abraham (Gal. 3:29).

The writer to the Hebrews finished his list of the basic teachings of Christ by mentioning the "resurrection of the dead" and "eternal judgment." It will help you greatly if you understand that both resurrection and judgment have a quality that is PAST and PRESENTLY PROGRESSIVE as well as FUTURE.

The point is that we must preach more than basic

salvation. It is not enough to see folks converted.
Believers must mature! There are far too many spiritual
dwarfs in our local churches. "O God, give us pastors
after your own heart (Jer. 3:15) which shall feed your
people with knowledge and understanding!" The Greek
word for "PASTOR" is "POIMEN" and means "a
SHEPHERD-FEEDER." It is translated 17 times in
the New Testament as "shepherd" and one time as
"pastor" (Eph. 4:11). The primary responsibility of a
pastor is to FEED, and to lay down his life for the sheep
(Jn. 10:1-16). He is to equip the saints to do the work of
the ministry. Sheep beget sheep. Shepherds reproduce
shepherds. We must train God's people, and show them
that salvation is a progressive truth ever unfolding in
their lives.

We must teach God's people that Jesus is Priest and
King. If we stop with the priestly principle, we will
produce frustrated sheep, because God has programmed
us with His own nature. And God is love. Do you
remember the law of love? The principle of love is
GIVING (Jn. 3:16). Don't let anyone tell you who are
genuinely converted (but have yet to taste of the Feast
of Pentecost) that the Holy Spirit is not working in your
life. He was the One who drew you to Jesus in the first
place (Jn. 6:44). The fruit of the Spirit is love (Gal. 5:22).
And this love of God is:

"Shed abroad in our hearts by the Holy Ghost"
(Rom. 5:5).

*"God's love floods our hearts through the Holy
Spirit" (Moffatt).*

*"Because the love of God has poured forth in our
hearts" (Broadus).*

He might not have come forth yet in all His
dimensions, but the Holy Ghost is working in the lives of

every born-again believer. We have been birthed of that nature, and that nature is working in us. Many of us have been filled with the Holy Ghost. God has sent forth the Spirit of His Son into our hearts (Gal. 4:6). CHRIST IN YOU, the hope of glory (Col. 1:25-29)! The manifestation of that Spirit in you will demonstrate Himself in love, giving, pouring forth, unselfishness, compassion, sacrifice . . . a living sacrifice (Rom. 12:1-2)! And all without somebody getting on an Egyptian "foot-pump" for 45 minutes . . . without "preaching" at you . . . without psychic pressure. God is bringing forth a people who do not come to church to be blessed or to have a "good time." Like their Master, they have come to minister and to give of the Life from within (Mk. 10:45)! The Holy Ghost is teaching us to become givers . . . He has laid a foundation in us and is now ready to go on to maturity!

WE ARE BEING SAVED

We have found a liberty in Christ. We have met Him Who is the Truth, and He is making us free (Jn. 8:32). There is a continual operation of His liberating influence upon us. We are being made (Rev. 1:6). We have learned to relate to Jesus as Priest and King. We understand that He is Lord and demands our life. I love His Presence more than His presents. I love the Giver more than the gifts. I love the God of the promise more than the promise. I love the God of heaven more than I love heaven. I love the God of the Bible more than I love the Bible. That is the first basic principle for the overcomer. Now we turn our attention to our second point: salvation is an experience that is progressive. There is a quality of salvation that is once-for-all. It is also true that we are BEING SAVED. In fact, we have been saved, we are being saved, and we shall be saved! Our SPIRIT has been saved, our SOUL is being saved, and our BODY shall be saved.

*"And the very God of peace sanctify you
WHOLLY; and I pray God your whole SPIRIT and
SOUL and BODY be preserved blameless unto the
coming of our Lord Jesus Christ. Faithful is He that
calleth you, Who will also do it" (1 Thess. 5:23).*

Man is a three-part being. Man is a trichotomy:
something with three parts. Man, like God, is in three
dimensions. Father, Son, Holy Ghost . . . spirit, soul, and
body. A tremendous study would be to open truths
concerning GOD'S Spirit, Soul, and Body! But we want
to keep this simple. There is another verse that reveals
man's constitution and make-up:

*"For the Word of God is quick, and powerful, and
sharper than any twoedged sword, piercing even to
the dividing asunder of SOUL and SPIRIT, and of
the joints and marrow, and is a discerner of the
THOUGHTS and INTENTS of the heart" (Heb.
4:12).*

The Word of God is quick. That doesn't mean fast;
rather, the Word is LIVING! That is because the Word
of God is a PERSON (Jn. 1:1-4)! You see, a word is the
expression of a thought. In order to have a thought, you
need a Thinker. The Father is a Thinker. The Father
thought, and then the Father spoke. And from the
bosom of the Father, the Word came forth and was made
flesh and tabernacled among us (Jn. 1:14-18). God was
manifest in the FLESH (1 Tim. 3:16).

This Living Word is a "discerner" (Greek is "critical,
discriminating, passing judgment; decisive") of the
THOUGHTS and INTENTS. The thoughts belong to
the realm of soul (or mind) and the intents belong to the
realm of spirit. Only the Word of the Living God can
divide (Greek is "to part, apportion, disunite, separate,
or distribute") soul and spirit. Man is a three-part being.
I will say more about soul and spirit later. We will see

how this relates to our theme. So many people have no joy. They are not overcomers because they are not growing. They are not maturing or developing in Christ Jesus because of a way of thinking. Their frame of mind is bent out of shape. Grace will cover and fit over anything, but their bumps and ridges are protruding from a traditional mentality. Listen to their confession:

"I AM SAVED!"

"I AM SAVED AND SANCTIFIED!"

"I AM SAVED AND SANCTIFIED AND FILLED WITH THE HOLY GHOST!"

Can you hear what they are saying? We are saved ... period. We are saved and sanctified ... period. We are saved and sanctified and filled with the Holy Ghost ... period. Whenever or wherever you put that "period" in your thinking, you automatically cut off any further revelation to your spirit. You will stop growing. I meet people from across the Body of Christ, and I have never met one yet who didn't say that he wanted to become more like Jesus. We all have said that. Our theology, our beliefs, our traditions result in our preventing ourselves from becoming what we say we want to be! Hence the conflict, the frustration, the unhappiness. The devil stands to the side and laughs. He only fears the overcomer.

Learn that Jesus is Priest and King. Learn that salvation *has* happened to you, *is* happening to you, and *shall* happen to you. Don't cut off the move of God from your life because of some stupid teaching. At least, be noble about it first (Acts 17:11). Don't commit spiritual suicide! If you examine truth by the Word, it will become stronger; if you examine tradition by the Word, it will fall apart.

SALVATION IS A COMPLETE DELIVERANCE

Salvation is a complete deliverance. Man is spirit, soul, and body. And the blood-bought redemption of the Lord Jesus Christ is all-inclusive, making provision for a complete deliverance of man's spirit, soul, and body. The Greek word for "SALVATION" is "SOTERIA" (#4991 in Strong's) and is used 45 times in the New Testament. The verb form is "SOZO" (#4982) and is used 111 times. This word is a misnomer. It is a misunderstood word. Perhaps this word study will clarify our Biblical terminology:

1. "Deliverance, preservation, salvation" (Vine's Dict. of N.T. Words).

2. "Deliverance, protection, made whole, health" (Strong's Concordance).

3. "Deliverance, preservation, safety, salvation" (Thayer's Lexicon).

Thus SALVATION means to be delivered. The new birth is the beginning of that deliverance. You and I will not be completely saved or delivered until this BODY experiences a redemption (Rom. 8:14-25). If you are not aware of this basic principle, you are the kind of person that breaks my heart. I want God's best for your life! Each Christian has such a beautiful potential for Jesus but will never realize it or walk in it unless he gets his eyes open to this truth. The most miserable people in the world are older folk who know that they missed it in their youth. God gave them an opportunity and a privilege to walk with Him, but they blew it! The lust of the flesh, the lust of the eyes, and the pride of life (1 Jn. 2:15-17) meant more to them than Jesus. Now they have a far-away look in their eyes. They will never experience the best of what they might have had in Him. Many have married outside of the will of God because of lust, and not love, and have made their bed in hell (Psa. 139:8).

They married the wrong person and now they are miserable. God stirred the hearts of many men and women to be part of a more excellent ministry, but a love of money and a life of comfort proved to be their god. Now they are miserable. If I have one prayer for you it is this: I want to see GOD'S BEST in your life! I want to see you come to your maximum potential in Jesus Christ! Don't settle for second or third best! Don't be content to die and go to heaven. An overcomer is one who comes over something. Come over what the religious systems have fed you. Come over your own pride. Come over your longing to build a reputation for your name. Come over into the Kingdom of God and a realm of complete deliverance. We have been delivered, we are being delivered, and we shall be delivered!

Somebody said, "Varner, I don't believe that there are three dimensions to salvation." Well, would you believe the Bible?

> "Who DELIVERED us from so great a death, and DOTH DELIVER: in whom we trust that he WILL yet DELIVER us" (2 Cor. 1:10).

> "Who rescued and saved us . . . and He will still rescue and save us . . . He will again deliver us" (The Amplified Bible).

> "It is He who has preserved us, and is preserving us, from such deadly peril" (Knox).

> ". . . on whom we have set our hope that He will also still deliver us" (American Standard).

> "Yes, and I expect Him to do it again and again" (Living Bible).

Who delivered us . . . what tense is that? When did God deliver you from so great a death, and what was so great a death?

"And you hath He quickened, who were DEAD in trespasses and sins . . . and hath raised us up together" (Eph. 2:1,6).

When you were initially saved, God delivered your SPIRIT. It is common Bible knowledge that a person who is a sinner without God, unconverted, unregenerated, is a person who lives in a state of SPIRITUAL death. That describes those who have yet to taste of the blood atonement of Jesus Christ to cover their sin. There is DEATH in the realm of SPIRIT . . . spiritual death!

When God first made Adam, there was LIFE in Adam's spirit. I know this because Adam COMMUNED with God (Gen. 1:26-31; 2:15-16; 3:8). God is a SPIRIT and we must worship Him in the realm of SPIRIT and truth (Jn. 4:23-24). You cannot worship God in the realm of soul (or mind). God bypasses your intellect, emotions, and will. I cannot and you cannot understand with our human reasonings the Mind of God. And we cannot understand the Book that He wrote, for that, too, must be SPIRITUALLY discerned (1 Cor. 2:9-14)! He that comes to God must believe that He IS (Heb. 11:6). That is not logical. Faith is contrary to reason, and faith is a SPIRITUAL force! The Bible makes no attempt to prove the existence of God . . . it assumes it! So before the transgression and the fall of man, Adam communed with God in the realm of the spirit. The spirit of man is that part of man that is GOD-conscious. You cannot know God in your mind. You must know Him in your spirit.

When Adam sinned, the result of that fall was SPIRITUAL DEATH (Gen. 3:1-24 and Rom. 5:12-21). A shroud of death and darkness came upon Adam's spirit. He still had a spirit, but it was DEAD UNTO GOD! Then death began to work in his mind and body. This is the condition that you and I were in when the Lord found us (Eph. 2:1). We lived in a realm void of His fellowship. No communion. No worship. Our spirits were dead unto God. And then:

> "The SPIRIT of man is the CANDLE of the Lord... That was the true Light, which lighteth every man, that cometh into the world. He was in the world, and the world was made by him, and the world knew him not... Then spake Jesus again unto them, saying, 'I am the LIGHT of the world: he that followeth me shall not walk in darkness, but shall have the light of life' " (Prov. 20:27; Jn. 1:9-10; 8:12).

When we were born from above (Jn. 3:1-8), Jesus the Light lit our candle! Our SPIRIT was raised from the dead (Eph. 2:6) and was passed from death unto life. Did you know that you have been resurrected? Praise His Name (Jn. 5:24)! So now every born-again believer has access to God in the realm of SPIRIT (Eph. 2:18). Now we can praise Him and love Him and have fellowship with Him! Our spirit has been delivered. We have been saved. We hear the testimony, "God saved my soul." No, God saved your spirit. Your soul is BEING saved. Somebody says, "It doesn't make any difference." It will if this truth is birthed in you! The living Word makes that difference and distinction (Heb. 4:12).

Let us learn to speak the same thing... the language of the Bible (1 Cor. 1:10). Most Christians are not aware of the difference between the soul and the spirit. We do not condemn those who do not know this (Heb. 5:2), but pray that their eyes will be enlightened to this basic truth for the overcomer (Eph. 1:18). We will never be that overcoming Church He desires if we do not conform to His image. We cannot be made like unto our Elder Brother if we do not see our need of being changed. We will not be changed until we learn that salvation is progressive!

Your spirit has been saved. Your candle has been lit

and your light can shine (Matt. 5:14)! We have passed
from death unto life. The new birth is an experience of
the power of His resurrection. And let's not get hung up
on that term: "new birth." For in truth we have been
born, we are BEING born (1 Pet. 1:23) and we SHALL
BE birthed (Rev. 12:1-5)! As noted, there are three
dimensions to this power of His resurrection. You and I
have already experienced a resurrection! We have been
raised from the state of spiritual death and passed into a
state of spiritual life. WE HAVE DIED AND GONE TO
HEAVEN TO BE WITH THE LORD (Eph. 2:1-6)!! We
have been birthed into the heavenlies!

Then there is a resurrection that is presently
progressive. It is saving and delivering us. Salvation is
progressive:

> *"And if the Spirit of Him Who raised up Jesus from
> the dead dwells in you, [then] He Who raised up
> Christ Jesus from the dead will also restore to life
> your mortal (short-lived, perishable) bodies through
> His Spirit Who dwells in you... [For my
> determined purpose is] that I may know Him—that
> I may PROGRESSIVELY become more deeply and
> intimately acquainted with Him, perceiving and
> recognizing and understanding [the wonders of His
> Person] more strongly and more clearly. And that I
> may in that same way come to know the POWER
> OUTFLOWING FROM HIS RESURRECTION
> [which it EXERTS over believers]; and that I may
> so share His sufferings as to be continually
> transformed [in spirit into His likeness even] to His
> death, [in the hope] That if possible I may attain to
> the [SPIRITUAL and MORAL] RESURRECTION
> [that lifts me] out from AMONG the dead [even
> while in the body]. Not that I have now attained
> [this ideal] or am already made perfect, but I PRESS
> ON to lay hold of (grasp) and make my own, that for
> which Christ Jesus, the Messiah, has laid hold of me*

*and made me His own . . . straining forward to what
lies ahead, I PRESS ON toward the goal to win the
[supreme and heavenly] prize to which God in Christ
Jesus is calling us upward" (Rom. 8:11; Phil. 3:10-14
in the Amplified Bible).*

One thing is clear: in Paul's mind, salvation was
progressive as well as once-for-all. And he had the Mind
of Christ (1 Cor. 2:16; Phil. 2:1-5). He taught the principle
of resurrection in three dimensions: past, present, and
future. Have you discovered yet that God thinks in
THREES? Israel knew His acts, but Moses knew the
way that God thought (Psa. 103:7). There are a lot of
people today who know what God can do. But do we
know the way He thinks? This plan of salvation came
from His Mind, and it is past, presently progressive, and
future.

TO LIVE IS TO GROW—TO GROW IS TO CHANGE

Somebody says, "Thank you, Lord, for saving me!"
Which dimension are you talking about? I am not trying
to be picky. I am not trying to stereotype Christians. I
don't want to put people into spiritual slots when I use
these Bible terms to show you truth. But I have the
desire to communicate to your spirit this truth:

"BROTHERS AND SISTERS, WE MUST GROW UP
INTO HIM IN ALL THINGS!"

Christian friend, you have got to grow up. You have
got to change. You have got to develop. We hear the
reply, "But why must I change? I am saved. I am born
again. I am already saved, so don't tell me that I have to
repent and change!" That is a typical reaction of most
evangelicals, and the mentality of the majority of the
Spirit-filled ranks is narrower than that. Well, I know

that you are born again but I also know that you are not
completely saved yet! If you believe that the new birth is
the Alpha and Omega of the Christian experience, that's
O.K. I won't condemn you. If you want to live and die
that way, go ahead . . . that's your business. But I know
from the Word of God that the day when Jesus became
your Saviour was the first day of a wonderful WALK
with your Redeemer. We want it . . . we want it
all . . . and then we want it all right now! No! There is no
ONE experience in this walk that does it all for you.
There are those who get overly excited and out of
balance in one area of truth, but this thing must be
worked out and walked out in the WHOLE counsel of
God (Acts 20:27). We are progressively learning to walk
in ALL the words of His Life and Kingdom (Acts 5:20).
And the Bible teaches that ALL that God does for you,
and ALL that you experience in this walk is your
salvation!

I am reminded of an Old Testament example of this. In
Ex. 27:1-8 God gave instruction to build the BRAZEN
ALTAR. It measured five by five by three cubits high. It
was the largest piece of furniture in the Tabernacle of
Moses. The Brazen Altar finds its complete antitype or
fulfillment in the CROSS of Christ. We all had our
beginnings at an old rugged Cross. The Tree of Life was
placed on the tree of death for each of us. Hallelujah!
This, then, in the Outer Court, was the place of our
beginnings. Now learn something. The Brazen Altar was
large enough to contain ALL the other pieces of
furniture in the Tabernacle. And in that Seed that was
deposited in each of us at birth is contained ALL that
the King IS and ALL that the King DOES! In every
born-again child of God, there is the Divine
POTENTIAL for ALL THINGS! Too many are
"claiming" their possessions . . . possess your possessions! There has been an IMPUTATION but there must
also be an IMPARTATION. The reality of His
Resurrection must be walked out in shoe leather! The

experience of justification by faith at the Brazen Altar makes you a candidate for all the fullness of God. But unless we grow up, we will remain servants in our experience though in His intended purpose we are lord of all (Gal. 3:29-4:1-7).

So the new birth is the BEGINNING of what God wants to do in your life. I know why so many Christians are miserable. I didn't say sinners. I said God's people. They are unhappy and frustrated because they still know their limitations. THERE IS STILL SIN IN THEIR LIFE AND THEY KNOW IT IS THERE! Then they come to church and somebody puts their arm around them and says, "It's all right, brother. You're saved." But you and I go on home and we KNOW that it is not all right! We need to change! The One on the inside telling us the truth is the same One that birthed us into this walk. And I would rather listen to the sweet Holy Ghost than some backslidden church member! You know why that hypocrite is telling you you're all right . . . because they are the same way (or worse) and God knows, if you change, they will have to change or look for the church of their choice. The minute you accept the truth that salvation is progressive, you start a spiritual chain reaction. You necessitate CHANGE! We must then grow and develop as part of the corporate Man that God is constructing to rule the earth (Eph. 4:13).

Salvation has a progressive quality. That is just another way of saying that God is doing something in my life TODAY! There is something fresh and vibrant and alive going on in us today! Jesus warned of "vain repetitions" (Matt. 6:7). Listen to some translations of that verse:

> "*Do not repeat the same words over and over again*" *(Twentieth Century).*

> "*Do not repeat empty phrases*" *(Goodspeed).*

*"You must not keep on repeating set phrases"
(Williams).*

"Do not go babbling on" (New English Bible).

*"Do not repeat the same thing over and over as the
pagans do" (Wuest).*

"Do not pray by idle rote like pagans" (Moffatt).

*"Don't recite the same prayer over and over as the
heathen do" (Taylor).*

The above is not only a Scriptural critique on some
"so-called" testimony meetings, but it is also a vivid
description of the lives of many believers. Testimonies
and lives that are twice dead, plucked up by the roots
(Jude 12). No fruit. All talk and no walk. I call that a
"Gilgal" testimony. Gilgal means "the place of the
circle." God is tired of testimonies that sound like a
broken record.

I don't want to know what you were prior to your
conversion. There is no life in it! Yet people gather
regularly to hear words of death. I guess they want some
soulish goose-bumps raised on their spiritually folded
arms. Just a bunch of spiritual "peeping toms" who
want to know what you and I were before we knew the
Lord. What made a man great in the Kingdom of
darkness does not make a man great in the Kingdom of
God! Faith comes by hearing the Word of Life and not a
testimony of death (Rom. 10:17). Thank God that many
are waking up. They are tired of eating on husks. They
are weary of trying to digest an empty shell with no corn
in it or any germ of life in it. It is none of your business
what I was prior to conversion and it is none of my
business what you were! Can't we just praise HIM that
HE has forgiven us and FORGOTTEN what we were?
Glory! Don't lift the lid on what the blood has covered (1
Sam. 6:19). It will kill you.

Most folk want to know what we WERE or what we WILL BE. They lust after past or future blessings because they are not victorious in the NOW. I repeat something I said in the previous message: the devil doesn't care what you believe, as long as it is in the past or the future! I want to stir you to say, "Lord, I want Your best for my life! I want to change NOW. There are some things in my life that need to be saved NOW. I need deliverance NOW." So I am not interested in your past, for this new order of ministry has no spiritual pedigree (Heb. 7:3). I want to know what God is doing in your life NOW ... TODAY! Be encouraged from the past. Have hope for the future. But be an overcomer in the present!

WE HAVE NOT BEEN EMPTIED FROM VESSEL TO VESSEL

"Moab has been at ease from his youth, and he has settled on his lees [like wine], and has not been drawn off from one vessel to another, neither has he gone into exile; therefore his taste remains in him and his scent HAS NOT CHANGED. Therefore, behold, the days are coming, says the Lord, when I shall send to [Moab] TILTERS who shall TILT him up, and shall empty his vessels and break his [earthenware] bottles in pieces. And Moab shall be ashamed..." (Jer. 48:11-13 in the Amplified Bible).

Jeremiah gives us the example of Moab to show us the kind of folk who will not believe that salvation is progressive. Moab will not change! If you do change and move with God, some will label you as a "compromiser," but what worked yesterday in our churches will not work today! Don't get too "settled." Don't bog down. This is serious. If we refuse to change, God will send messengers that will tip and tilt Moab's vessel. Do you remember when Jesus "tipped" some tables (Jn. 2:13-17; Mt. 21:12-13)? If we are not willing to change, then God will eventually bring judgment . . . He will change us one way or the other. Moab "hath not been EMPTIED from vessel to vessel" (KJV). This describes the process of PURIFYING wine. There was a constant pouring out of the wine into another container and a drawing off of the impurities. After each step, the wine became SWEETER and CLEARER. The message comes through: we are being changed as God pours us from one realm of glory to another (2 Cor. 3:18)! From faith to faith (Rom. 1:17) and from strength to strength (Psa. 84:7) we are being saved.

But there are those who refuse to be poured out. They have no desire to be a container and then a dispenser for the Wine of God's Holy Ghost (Acts 2:17; Psa. 104:15). They have not gone to the place of captivity where they are bound by a Covenant of love (Acts 28:20). But they sure do want God to pour the wine in! And they want to get drunk on it so they can do their own thing (Judg. 21:25). Their scent has not changed. The same old cabbage is their weekly fare. But God is changing our diet (Josh. 5:12)! It is a diet for conquerors and overcomers who are going to rise up in faith and possess the land.

Let God pour you out. Some of you wouldn't mind that as long as all the bottles are ALIKE! We will change from church to church as long as they are teaching the SAME thing, or as long as they are in the SAME movement. But what if God says, "I am going to put you in this RECTANGULAR bottle." "But, God, I am ROUND. I have been ROUND all my life. My mother was ROUND. My whole family is ROUND. I am NOT going to be RECTANGULAR! I want to be ROUND!"

So what does God do with the man or woman who stubbornly refuses to change? He waits . . . He waits. He has all the time in the world . . . but you don't! Then just about the time we have adjusted to that ROUND bottle,

God says, "You have been round long enough. Let me empty you into the SQUARE vessel." There is only one way that we keep up with Him and continue to flow with Him: we must understand that salvation is progressive!

God wants us to walk with Him. There was one thing in the Garden of Eden that is missing in present-day Christianity: a WALK with God (Gen. 3:8). Stop living in the past! He has brought you out that He might bring you into a life that drips with His victory. But you will have to be poured out and emptied from vessel to vessel.

I WILL MEET WITH THEE YET A THIRD TIME

God's program is in THREES . . . remember? There is an interesting word in an interesting Scripture that bears out this principle:

> *"That thy trust may be in the Lord, I have made known to thee this day, even to thee. Have not I written to thee EXCELLENT THINGS in counsels and knowledge, that I might make thee know the certainty of the words of truth; that thou mightest answer the words of truth to them that send unto thee" (Pr. 22:19-21).*

The word "EXCELLENT," as used here, is the Hebrew word "shalish" meaning THREE-FOLD, or weighty. From the same root come other words given as "captain, or lord, or great measure." As a captain it refers to ONE OF, OR OVER THREE. "Have I not written unto you THREE-FOLD things?" Three-fold things. These are the excellent things of God. These are weighty things. This threefold principle is brought forth again and again as the Spirit unfolds the truth so desperately needed for this hour.

God has promised to meet with man in three dimensions. He has met man historically and experientially in the first and second realms. I declare to you that He will meet with us historically and experientially yet a THIRD time!

> *"THREE TIMES in a year shall all thy males appear before the Lord thy God in the place which HE shall choose; in the feast of UNLEAVENED BREAD, and in the feast of WEEKS, and in the feast of TABERNACLES: and they shall not appear before the Lord empty" (Deut. 16:16).*

God will meet with man THREE times. The Feast of Unleavened Bread is another name for the Feast of PASSOVER. The Feast of Weeks is another name for the Feast of PENTECOST. And then comes the Feast of TABERNACLES. These feasts that took place in the Old Testament economy of a natural people are types and shadows of a true and real spiritual experience for the individual believer and for the Body of Christ as a whole. There is both an individual and a corporate aspect to the feasts.

When God meets man in the first dimension, He meets us in the Feast of Passover. Jesus is SAVIOUR in that realm. When I see the blood, I will pass over you (Ex. 12:13)! Christ our Passover is sacrificed for us. Jesus is the Lamb of God. He was slain from the foundation of the world. His blood is precious (1 Cor. 5:7; Jn. 1:29; Rev. 13:8; 1 Pet. 1:18-19)!

Has God met with you for the first time? Have you eaten the Lamb? If so, the Lamb is WITHIN you! And the Lamb from within will speak to you in the Feast of Unleavened Bread. We must know the reality of having His BLOOD applied to the doorpost of our heart. Then, when the messenger of death and destruction passes through the land, we will be safe behind the blood-stained wooden Door (Jn. 10:7).

The Feast of Pentecost was a separate feast and the pentecostal experience is a separate experience. Has God met with you a second time? God does not stop at Pentecost and the second feast is the earnest and the firstfruits of the final feast (Rom. 8:23; Eph. 1:13-14). Pentecost is NOT the fullness. Tabernacles is the fullness! The third feast is a HARVEST feast and a Feast of Ingathering. In the first dimension, He is JESUS, the Saviour. In the second dimension, He is CHRIST, the Anointed One. But in the third dimension, He is LORD, the Lord of the harvest!

There are a lot of folks who want to have a "meeting in the air" (1 Th. 4:17) (and there will be one) who have only met with the Lord once. That is something to think about. Paul said that there would be a GLORIOUS CHURCH (Eph. 5:25-27) or a Church that radiates His GLORY! That kind of people will have experienced not one, not two, but THREE Feasts, for the Feast of Tabernacles was the feast of the appearing of the glory of the Lord.

I am coming back to this thought of three-fold things later. I mention it now to show you yet another way of discerning that salvation is progressive. My spirit has been saved, my SOUL is being saved, and my body shall be saved. Now I want to explain more fully the truth that my soul is BEING saved. This is a real key to our understanding of God's purpose. Every overcomer must know this.

BE TRANSFORMED BY
THE RENEWING OF YOUR MIND

In order to understand the saving of the SOUL, we must know that the SOUL is:

1. Man's INTELLECT—what we THINK—our OPINIONS.

2. Man's EMOTIONS—what we FEEL—our FEELINGS.

3. Man's WILL—what we WANT—our DESIRES.

To this could be added the ATTITUDES of man. God is saving our attitudes! We could simplify the soulish realm into one word: MIND. The terms soulish mind, and CARNAL mind, and natural mind are synonymous. Interestingly enough, the Latin word for "MEAT" is "CARNE." An animal that is CARNIVOROUS is a MEAT-eater. The CARNAL mind is a MEATHEAD! No wonder God wants to save it! This is a key verse:

> *"Do not be conformed to this world—this age, fashioned after and adapted to its external, superficial customs. But be TRANSFORMED (changed) by the [entire] RENEWAL OF YOUR MIND—by its new ideals and its new ATTITUDE —so that you may prove [for yourselves] what is the good and acceptable and perfect will of God, even the thing which is good and acceptable and perfect [in His sight for you]" (Rom. 12:2 in the Amplified Bible).*

> *"But let God remold your minds from within" (Phillips).*

> *"But be transforming yourselves by the renewing of your mind" (Rotherham).*

> *"And stop assuming an outward expression that does not come from WITHIN you and is not representaive of what you ARE in your INNER BEING ... but change your outward expression to one that comes from WITHIN and is representative of your INNER BEING, by the renewing of your mind" (Wuest's Expanded Translation).*

Change your outward expression (your circumstances) to be in accord with the One within (Col. 1:27). Be transforming yourselves! We have been PURCHASED and we have been PURPOSED: we have been TRANS-LATED out of darkness and into the Light; (1 Pet. 2:9-10; Col. 1:12-13) now we must TRANSFORM ourselves by the renewing of our mind! GOD has brought you out of ignorance. The purpose of the ministries of Eph. 4:11 is to get you to CHANGE YOUR MIND! Learn this:

"THE GREATEST HINDRANCE TO YOUR CHRISTIAN WALK IS THE WAY THAT YOU THINK!"

The devil is not your problem. It's what you THINK about the devil! Circumstances are not the issue, but rather what we THINK about those circumstances. Let us give ear and submit our minds to the LIVING WORD that is coming through God's prophets in this hour. We must stop thinking like men and start thinking like sons of God!

The word for "TRANSFORMED" in Rom. 12:2 is the Greek word "METAMORPHOO" (#3339 in Strong's) and means simply "to change into another form" (Vine). Compare the example of the METAMORPHOSIS of the worm to the butterfly. It comes from two words:

1. META—implying CHANGE.

2. MORPHE—form.

This word is used but 4 times in the New Testament. In Matt. 17:2 and Mk. 9:2 it is given as "TRANSFIGURED" and in 2 Cor. 3:18 it is rendered as "CHANGED."

There is a transformation, a transfiguration that is presently taking place in our lives and this change is in our MINDS. We limit God by the way that we THINK.

*"For as he THINKETH in his heart (Hebrew is
"soul"), so is he" (Prov. 23:7).*

*"For as he hath thought in his soul, so is he"
(Young's Literal).*

*"For as he reckoneth within himself, so is he"
(Revised Version).*

*"For just as he hath thought in his own mind, so is
he" (Rotherham).*

The devil is not your problem. It's what you THINK
about the devil! The way that we THINK about a
certain thing will determine what we SAY and DO about
it. It will determine what we ARE!
    You need to *change your mind.* It is a matter of life or
death, for:

*". . . those who are according to the FLESH and
controlled by its unholy desires, set their MINDS on
and pursue those things which gratify the flesh. But
those who are according to the Spirit and [controlled
by the desires] of the Spirit, set their MINDS on and
seek those things which gratify the (Holy) Spirit.*

*Now the MIND OF THE FLESH [which is SENSE
and REASON without the Holy Spirit] is
DEATH—death that comprises all the miseries
arising from sin, both here and hereafter. But the
MIND OF THE (HOLY) SPIRIT is life and soul-
peace [both now and forever]. [That is] because the
MIND OF THE FLESH—with its CARNAL
THOUGHTS AND PURPOSES—is hostile to God;
for it does not submit itself to God's law, indeed it
cannot.*

So then those who are living the life of the

> *FLESH—catering to the appetites and impulses of their CARNAL NATURE—cannot please or satisfy God, or be acceptable to him" (Rom. 8:5-8 —Amplified).*

To be carnally minded is DEATH! To be spiritually minded is LIFE and PEACE! If you think like a MAN, you will think death and talk death. If you will think like GOD, you will think life and talk life! When I speak of DEATH, I am not referring to a termination of physical life, I am speaking of the REALM of death (negativism) . . . anything that is temporal (2 Cor. 4:17-18) or contrary to the living Word of God! The realm of death is the realm of FEAR and DARKNESS and IGNORANCE and BONDAGE and LIMITATION and SORROW. These things are on the MINDS of MEN. The man who walks after the flesh walks after his five natural senses. The world system is going mad because they are governed by their natural eyes and ears. Men's hearts are failing them for FEAR (Lk. 21:26). The enemy has deceived the whole world through FEAR (Rev. 12:9-10). The carnal mind walks by SIGHT and not by faith (2 Cor. 5:7; Rom. 14:23).

ENOCH WAS TRANSLATED
THAT HE SHOULD NOT SEE DEATH

Everything outside of the Christ nature is a lying vanity. That which men call life is really death . . . it is passing away. But that which is of God is eternal and permanent. The realm of the SPIRIT is the real world! We who are the children and heirs of God are not to think like the world. We are not to act like the world. We have by-passed our human "genius" and have heard something in the realm of FAITH! God has a people in the earth that have seen the realm of SPIRIT! Death is not working in them, but rather the Life of the Christ from within. Let us not bind this Strong Man within us. There is an endless increase that flows from Him and His Kingdom has no limitation (Isa. 9:6-7).

It is seen in the listing of the nine gifts or manifestations of the Spirit that Christians are to be SUPER-natural people, for (1 Cor. 12:8-10):

1. Through the SPEAKING MINISTRY of the VOCAL gifts (prophecy, and divers kinds of tongues, and interpretation of tongues), we can SAY things that NATURAL men cannot say. We can SPEAK like God!

2. Through the KNOWING MINISTRY of the REVELATION gifts (the word of wisdom, the word of knowledge, and the discerning of spirits), we can KNOW things that NATURAL men cannot know. We can THINK like God!

3. Through the DOING MINISTRY of the POWER gifts (faith, working of miracles, and the gifts of healings), we can DO things that NATURAL men cannot do. We can ACT like God (do the WORKS of God)!

The world is going crazy, and we are talking about righteousness, peace, and joy in the Holy Ghost! Many people are talking about how bad it is and how DARK it is getting. Hogwash! It might be getting dark where you live, but:

"... the path of the JUST is as the SHINING LIGHT, that shineth MORE and MORE unto the perfect day" (Prov. 4:18).

"But the path of the righteous is as the light of dawn, going on and brightening, unto meridian day" (Rotherham).

". . . which shines brighter and brighter until full day" (RSV).

". . . that grows in brilliance till perfect day" (New American Standard).

"The course of good men, like a ray of dawn, shines on and on to the full light of day" (Moffatt).

". . . going on and brightening till the day is established" (Young's Lit.).

"But the good man walks along in the ever-brightening light of God's favor; the dawn gives way to morning splendor" (Living Bible).

"But the path of the uncompromisingly just and righteous is like the light of dawn, that shines more and more—brighter and clearer—until [it reaches its FULL STRENGTH and glory in] the perfect (to-be-prepared) day" (The Amplified Bible).

The Day of the Lord IS dark and gloomy. But it is also like the MORNING that is spread upon the mountains (Joel 2:1-2). Darkness SHALL cover the earth, but the GLORY of the Lord will be seen upon His Church (Isa. 60:1-5). This Day is burning like an oven, but to those who fear God, He is rising with HEALING in His wings! We have nothing to fear (Mal. 4:1-3)! Isaiah said for us to ARISE! Shake off your bitterness and resentment. Get out of your fear and unbelief. This is not of God. It has hurt you too long and it will kill you.

Salvation is progressive. The Light is shining more and more. God is bringing forth a people who are blind to a realm of death. Their eyes have been opened to behold HIM, and He is Life!

"By FAITH Enoch was TRANSLATED that HE

SHOULD NOT SEE DEATH; and WAS NOT FOUND, because God had translated him: for BEFORE his translation he had this testimony, that he PLEASED God" (Heb. 11:5).

Enoch was translated into a realm where he did not SEE the realm of death. He could not relate to a realm of death (Gen. 5:20-24; Lk. 3:37; Jude 14). God has a schedule that is only interrupted by faith, and Enoch walked in the powers of an age to come (Heb. 6:5). Enoch was the SEVENTH from Adam. "One day is with the Lord as a thousand years" (2 Pet. 3:8). We are moving into the SEVENTH day from ADAM, and the THIRD day from JESUS. Once again, somebody will be translated that they should not see death! But without FAITH, it is impossible to please Him.

Enoch could not be found! Likewise, we are dead and our life is HID away with Christ in God (Col. 3:1-3). The first one who will notice that you are missing out from among the fearful and unbelieving is the devil. He is seeking after you, but he cannot find you (1 Pet. 5:8; Jn. 14:30). He cannot devour the people who with Paul in 2 Cor. 4:17-18 are looking at invisible things, the eternal things of the Spirit. There is a faith-walk in the Spirit for the overcomer, for:

"There is a PATH which no FOWL knoweth, and which the VULTURE'S eye hath not seen: the LION'S WHELPS have not trodden it, nor the FIERCE LION passed by it" (Job 28:7-8).

"No wild animal has ever walked upon those treasures; no lion has set his paw there" (The Living Bible).

"A path the vulture hath not discerned . . . ravenous beasts have not made a track thereof, neither hath the lion marched thereon" (Rotherham).

"No proud beast ever paces it, no lion moves along it" (Moffatt).

The devil is a dirty bird (Matt. 13:4,19; Mk. 4:15; Lk. 8:12). There is a highway (Isa. 35:1-10). There is a heavenly path. There is a high calling (Phil. 3:14). There is nothing on that path that interests the devil. The vulture is not interested, for he feeds upon DEATH. He feasts upon the death and sorrow and sickness and sin and poverty of those who live in the DUST (Gen. 3:14-19; Isa. 65:25). We cannot see the realm of death. Somebody says, "But it is getting so dark! The devil is running rough-shod over everybody! Look at the signs of the times!" I'm sorry, friend, but I can't see it! I am looking unto JESUS (Heb. 12:1-2) and His brilliance is so dazzling I am blind to anything else! I just cannot relate to a realm of death, for I have been translated into a realm of life. I am walking by faith and the lion's whelps (demons) have not trodden this path, nor the fierce lion passed by it!

THE END OF YOUR FAITH

Your soul is BEING saved. The SOUL is the intellect, emotions, and will of man; what he thinks, what he feels, and what he wants. God has saved your *spirit*, and now He is progressively delivering your soul. We have been saved, we are being saved, and we shall be saved. "But he that shall endure unto the END, the same shall be saved" (Matt. 24:13). Peter embraced this principle in his first epistle:

"Receiving the END of your faith, even the SALVATION of your SOULS" (1 Pet. 1:9).

". . . you receive the result (outcome, consummation) of your faith, the salvation of your souls" (The Amplified Bible).

"You are sure of the end to which your faith looks forward, that is the salvation of your souls" (Jerusalem Bible).

"... to obtain the outcome of your faith" (Moffatt).

"... the goal of your faith" (The Berkeley Version).

"... while you reap the harvest of your faith" (New English Bible).

"Receiving the promised consummation of your faith which is the [final] salvation of your souls" (Wuest's Expanded Translation).

Your soul is being saved. There are three other passages of Scripture that parallel the verse given above:

"In your PATIENCE possess ye your souls" (Lk. 21:19).

"Wherefore lay apart all filthiness and superfluity of naughtiness, and receive with meekness the engrafted word, which is able to SAVE your souls" (James 1:21).

"Now the just shall live by faith: but if any man draw back, my soul shall have no pleasure in him. But we are not of them who draw back unto perdition; but of them that BELIEVE TO THE SAVING OF THE SOUL" (Heb. 10:38-39).

The principles of PATIENCE and DISCIPLINE and ENDURANCE are evident here. We have learned that ENOCH was translated into a dimension where he did not see death. Enoch's name means "one who is initiated; to discipline, dedicate, or train up; narrow." It is training time for reigning time. And few there be that find it (Matt. 7:13-14).

The man who tells me his soul is already saved is also telling me his faith is ENDED! He doesn't believe that God will heal the sick. He doesn't believe that we can be filled with the Holy Ghost as in the Book of Acts. He doesn't believe in the laying on of hands. He does not believe in the gifts of the Spirit. He does not believe in the ministry gifts of apostles and prophets. He does not believe that he is Abraham's seed and an heir according to the promise. He does not believe that the church must come to maturity before Jesus can come a second time. His faith is ended! Somebody told him that he "got it all" when he was born again. The man who told him that was a fool, and the man who believed it was a fool. You may say, "How dare you talk that way to folks!" Should we ignore a groaning creation and let folks go ahead and wrap their arms around a lie that keeps them miserable? A lie that never lets them mature and come to their full potential in Jesus? I love people more than that! I love YOU more than that!

> *"Now, am I trying to win the favor of men, or of God? Do I seek to be a man-pleaser? If I were still seeking popularity with men, I should not be a bondservant of Christ, the Messiah ... the Gospel ... made known by me is not man's gospel—patterned after any human standard" (Gal. 1:10-11 in the Amplified Bible).*

Do you know WHY people love the traditions that keep them in a realm of stunted spiritual growth? Do you know WHY some are still making up their minds about this message? Do you know WHY some are having second thoughts about following this Gospel that proclaims Jesus to be Lord? Because they know what is going to happen the very minute that they say "Amen."

If a man says "I believe that Jesus is Priest and King.

I believe that my soul is being delivered. I believe that God needs to do a continual work of salvation in my mind, my emotions, my will, my attitudes, and my desires!" The moment that YOU or I say that is the moment we take upon ourselves the RESPONSIBIL-ITY of submitting to the working of the Holy Spirit to complete that work!

God's people have yet to learn that at initial salvation sin was cut off, but not cut out. AFTER the birth, we need to be CIRCUMCISED. And while it is true that WATER BAPTISM in the Name of the Lord is the outward seal of the New Covenant, just as CIR-CUMCISION was the outward seal of the Old Covenant (Gen. 17), there yet remains a need in each of our lives to be circumcised AGAIN (Josh. 5:2)! And do you understand that we have been circumcised, and WE ARE BEING CIRCUMCISED, and we shall be circum-cised? The pattern is consistent. There has *been* a cutting away, there *is* a cutting away, and there *shall be* a cutting away! God is cutting away MY mind and emotions and will that HIS Mind and emotions and will may develop. He is pruning MY soul-life so that HIS Soul-life can come forth. Do you want HIS opinions and feelings and desires to be your portion? Then know that YOUR soul-life must be dealt with. We must have an encounter with God!

Let me give you an example of this encounter. Every time we meet another person and progressively form a relationship, there is a MUTUAL EXCHANGE. After each encounter, we part, each taking some of the other with him. After you and I have met, you take some of ME with you, and I take some of YOU with me! A practical and helpful word of encouragement in passing: if you do not like someone else, perhaps it is because you do not KNOW that person. Get to know that other person, and get to know God! For, when you meet God and encounter HIS Person, something beautiful begins to happen! When you and I spend time with the Lord,

something beautiful CONTINUES to happen! A
transformation that is presently progressive works in
the renewing of our minds. We take more and more of
HIM, and He takes more and more of US!! In the words
of John the Baptist,

> *"He must INCREASE, but I must DECREASE"*
> *(Jn. 3:30).*

> *"He must grow greater, but I must grow less"*
> *(Weymouth).*

> *"It is necessary in the nature of the case for that*
> *One to become CONSTANTLY greater but for me*
> *CONSTANTLY to be made less" (Wuest).*

> *"He must grow more prominent, I must grow less*
> *so" (The Amplified Bible).*

> *"He must become greater and greater, and I must*
> *become less and less" (The Living Bible).*

There is an Old Testament principle that says the
same thing. Do you remember REBELLIOUS Saul and
REPENTANT David? They represent FLESH and
SPIRIT.

> *"Now there was LONG WAR between the house of*
> *Saul and the house of David: but David waxed*
> *STRONGER and STRONGER, and the house of*
> *Saul waxed WEAKER and WEAKER ... for the*
> *FLESH lusteth against the SPIRIT, and the Spirit*
> *against the flesh: and these are CONTRARY the*
> *one to the other" (2 Sam. 3:1; Gal. 5:17).*

> *"And these are entrenched in an attitude of mutual*
> *opposition" (Wuest).*

I cannot speak for you, but there are things about my
intellect that are wrong. There are some things about my
emotions that have yet to be healed or saved. There are
some things about my will that get in His way. I have
some wrong attitudes. I know that all my desires are not
Christ-like. I am honest enough to tell you that I
desperately need more of Jesus Christ in my life! I need
more of His Word. I need more of His Spirit. I need more
of His working. I need more of His deliverance. I NEED
MORE OF HIS SALVATION!!

We have not arrived. If you think you have, then pray
for me! We haven't made it yet. Salvation is progressive.
Don't wear two hats. Either you got it all when you were
born again, or you need some more. It can't be both
ways. I have said "Amen" to this truth, and I am
submitting my life to His Lordship and the dealings of
His Spirit. I have accepted this new-found responsibility. In so doing, I have laid on HIM the responsibility
to do a complete work in my life. We have become His
workmanship. You and I are His masterpiece. There is a
piece of the Master in each of us, and He is working in us
to will and to do of HIS good pleasure (Phil. 2:13).

*"The Lord will PERFECT that which
CONCERNETH ME: thy mercy, O Lord, endureth
for ever: forsake not the WORKS OF THINE OWN
HANDS ... being confident of this very thing, that
he which hath BEGUN a good WORK in you will
PERFORM IT until the day of Jesus Christ" (Psa.
138:8; Phil. 1:6).*

A GOAT-HAIR FEELING

Salvation is progressive. The soul is the intellect,
emotions, and will. My intellect is what I think. It is my
OPINION. Have you ever heard someone say, "Let me
tell you what I think! This is what I think about ..."?

That must change until ALL of us can say, "Let me tell you what HE thinks about it!" That's the Mind of Christ . . . God's way of thinking. God does not think the same way that a man does.

> *"Seek ye the Lord while he may be found, call ye upon him while he is near: Let the wicked forsake HIS way, and the unrighteous man HIS THOUGHTS . . . for My THOUGHTS are not your thoughts, neither are your ways My ways, saith the Lord. For as the heavens are higher than the earth, so are My ways higher than your ways, AND MY THOUGHTS THAN YOUR THOUGHTS"* (Isa. 55:6-9).

Let this Mind be in you (Phil. 2:5). And the Mind that was in Christ Jesus was the Mind of the Father! Men can only see with the natural eye, but God sees the end from the beginning (Isa. 46:10). His Mind is not governed by the five natural senses. At times, it is just not sensible to be led by His Spirit (Rom. 8:14). This message is not meant to be sensible. You cannot understand it with your intellect. You can only understand the truth with HIS intellect! The world system is ruled by men who are demon-possessed. It is interesting that the word "demon" means "a KNOWING ONE." The only way we can be victorius over these "intelligences" is for us to be clothed with a Higher Intelligence! The overcomer has relinquished his way of thinking that he might put on the Mind of Christ. Some have said, "This Kingdom message is new. We have never heard these things before. I believe that Varner has lost his mind." HE HAS! Glory! I am in good company, for the one who prophesied that the axe would be laid to the root of the tree (Matt. 3:10) felt the axe! John lost his head. His head was removed, for THE Head had come (Matt. 14:1-10). Thank God that He is saving our souls. We are learning to think like our Father. Our blinded minds have been transformed to an unveiled face, for our hearts have turned to the Lord (2 Cor. 3:14-18). We have lost our minds.

Secondly, the soul of man is his emotions...his feelings. Listen to the conversations of God's people and you will constantly hear, "How are you feeling? Oh, I feel..." Did you ever get a goat-hair feeling? Isaac did.

> *"And it came to pass, that when Isaac was old, and his eyes were dim, so that HE COULD NOT SEE... And Rebekah took goodly raiment of her eldest son Esau... and she put the SKINS of the kids of the GOATS upon his (Jacob's) hands... And Isaac said unto Jacob, 'Come near, I pray thee, THAT I MAY FEEL THEE, my son, whether thou be my very son Esau or not'... And he DISCERNED him not" (Gen. 27:1,15-16,21-23).*

Isaac was blind as a bat. And so is the man who is led by his feelings! Many are still throwing out "fleeces" and getting fleeced (Judg. 6:36-40). If you have not learned that God has written down His Mind in black and white... if the Spirit of God is not enough to guide you (Jn. 16:13)... if you must resort to the middle-ages mentality of the old order, then do what Gideon did. Make your fleece DOUBLY IMPOSSIBLE! For your sake, remember that somebody else may be listening.

A goat-hair feeling will fool you. Your feelings will cause you to miss it. I want you to learn to be an overcomer and discern the right way to go. But the way that some of us "feel" about certain things is ungodly; that is, we do not feel the same way that God does about it. Please understand that I am not doing what some of His servants have done: I am not doing away with feelings! I just want to exchange my perverted feelings for HIS Godly feelings. If you do away with feelings or emotions altogether, you will produce a bunch of spiritual zombies. I want to love as HE loves... I want to hate as HE hates (Prov. 6:16-19).

Thirdly, the soul of man is his will . . . his desires. We need to change. Our wants and desires need saving. As I noted in the previous message, that verse in Ps. 37:4 does NOT mean that God will give us what we want! It means, rather, that the very desires that are in us are HIS desires! We want what HE wants! We will what HE wills! We crave what HE craves!

There were three men in a boat: Jonah, Paul, and Jesus. Three men in a boat and three boats in a storm. One man was OUT of the will of God. One man was IN the will of God. The third Man WAS the will of God. Jonah was OVERCOME by the storm. Paul ENDURED the storm. But Jesus CONTROLLED the storm! And as He is, so are we (1 Jn. 4:17). There is a people who are becoming the will of God in the earth.

REPENTANCE IS NOT A BAD WORD

Repentance is a key to this progressive salvation. Can you imagine the reaction of the average Christian to this conversation?

"How was the service last night, Brother Varner? Did you get a blessing?"

"Yes . . . in a way."

"How is that?"

"I repented!"

"You mean, you went to the altar? I thought you were already saved."

"I am, but I am being saved. I didn't go to the altar . . . I changed my mind!"

I know that to most REPENTANCE is something that they did five years ago, or one year ago, or fifty years ago. There is more to this thing called repentance than you might realize. The first thing you must see is that repentance is not a bad word.

A quick word of balance: I am not speaking about

those people who get "saved" and "healed" and "delivered" every spring and fall. Nor am I speaking about the dear misguided saint who gets genuinely converted and is told that "ALL things have become new" (2 Cor. 5:17), only to discover that all things have NOT become new! In frustration he returns to the altar to get saved again and again and again . . .

Repentance is a blessed attitude that every believer who aspires to the overcoming life must WALK in. This thought will take us back to the principle of having your mind renewed. This concept of REPENTANCE is best introduced by a word study:

"REPENTANCE" = the Greek word METANOIA which means:

1. "Compunction (for guilt, including reformation); by implication, reversal (of [another's] decision); repentance; to think differently or afterwards; reconsider (feel compunction)"—Strong's (#3341).

2. "After-thought, change of mind; from META (after, implying change) and NOUS (the mind, the seat of moral reflection)"—Vine's Dictionary.

3. "An entire change of character, and a renunciation of all that is evil, by which renunciation we wish that evil void or undone"—Bengel.

4. "A thorough change of the heart and soul, of the life and actions"—Trench's Synonymns of the New Testament.

5. "A change of mind: as it appears in one who repents of a purpose he has formed or of something he has done"—Thayer's Lexicon.

REPENTANCE IS A CHANGE OF MIND.

Whenever you find the word "TURN" or "RETURN" in the Scriptures, this concept is usually involved. When Paul penned that passage in Rom. 12:1-2 he was saying, "Brothers and sisters, change your minds! Get it renewed. Start thinking differently. Don't think the way that you have in the past. Take on the thoughts of God which you will find in the Scriptures. The Word of God is His Mind and His thoughts. Stop thinking like men and start thinking like God!"

The truth of repentance is a broad truth. We are putting off the mind of the flesh and are putting on the Mind of Christ. Thus, repentance is the ENTIRE change of mind from a state of complete death to a state of fullness of life. Like salvation, repentance is progressive as well as once-for-all. Repentance is not a bad word. It encompasses and includes the entire change in the believer from conception to perfection. Repentance is an attitude and a way of life. Repentance is a progressive process. Repentance is an attitude that every believer needs in his spirit. The overcomer is a man who knows how to change his mind for God's Mind. King Saul is remembered as a REBELLIOUS man. King David was an adulterer and a murderer, but is known by all as the man after God's own heart. David knew how to REPENT (Psa. 51). May we not allow the pride and the stubbornness of our way to keep us from the glory of His Kingdom. Are we flexible? Can we bend? We ALL have sinned and come short of the glory of God (Rom. 3:23). Let us TURN from our way to the ways of the Lord (2 Chron. 7:14) that we may be healed and restored. Peter knew that repentance is a key to this present outpouring:

> *"Therefore repent at once, instantly CHANGING YOUR ATTITUDE, and perform a RIGHT-ABOUT-FACE in order that your sins may be obliterated, IN ORDER THAT there may come epoch-making periods of spiritual revival and*

*refreshment from the presence of the Lord, and in
order that He may send off on a mission to you
Christ Jesus who has been appointed, this
appointment being in the interest of your well-
being; Whom it is a necessity in the nature of the
case for HEAVEN indeed to receive UNTIL times
when all things will be restored to their pristine
glory, things regarding which God spoke through
the mouth of His holy prophets who lived in bygone
times ... And indeed, all the prophets since Samuel,
and those who followed, one after another, as many
as spoke, also announced these days" (Acts
3:19-21,24—Wuest).*

Jesus "must remain in heaven" (Goodspeed) until this
Scripture is fulfilled. (Compare Psa. 110:1; Eph. 4:13; Js.
5:7.) We must experience "epoch-making periods of
spiritual revival" before He can come! The Authorized
Version reads "REPENT ye therefore, and be
CONVERTED." That word "converted" is the Greek
word "epistrepho" and means "to turn about, turn
towards" (Vine). We must turn from OUR ways to HIS
way! The word "WHEN" in the King James is the word
"hopos" (#3704 in Strong's) and means "SO THAT, IN
ORDER THAT." Let us repent and turn to God SO
THAT, IN ORDER THAT the latter rain may fall!
Repentance is a key to this revival. Job knew this truth,
for he said that God:

*"... maketh small the drops of water, they pour
down rain according to the vapour thereof" (Job
36:27).*

*"They refine rain according to its vapour" (Young's
Literal Translation).*

As the vapour of our prayers go up to Him in
repentance, the rain will fall. No repentance, no rain on

our land (2 Chron. 7:14). So many in the church world are filled with fear. The reason that people are filled with fear is that for too long they have meditated on the words of the devil. Faith is a spiritual force and fear is a spiritual force. Faith comes by hearing the Words of God. Fear comes by hearing the words of the devil. Both faith and fear have a voice. Men are responsible for hearing the wrong voice, and they will have to repent of that! They must TURN from the wrong voice to the right Voice (Rom. 10:17)!

"Can two walk together, except they be agreed?" *(Amos 3:3).*

"Do two men travel together, unless they have planned it?" (Moffatt).

"For how can we walk together with your sins between us?" (Living Bible).

If you agree with the words of the devil, you walk with the devil. And if you agree with the words of God, you walk with God. You are walking and talking with the one that you agree with . . . a covenant of death or a covenant of life. For example, GOD said that by the stripes of Jesus, you are healed (Isa. 53:5; 1 Pet. 2:24)! The devil and the carnal mind says that God doesn't heal folks today and that it is God's will for people to be sick and suffering. GOD has said that He has sent His apostles, and prophets, and evangelists, and pastors, and teachers to perfect the Church and equip her to do the work of the ministry, to mature her until she comes to the measure of the stature of the fullness of Christ (Eph. 4:11-13). The devil and the carnal minds say that there are no apostles and prophets today and that the Church is ready to meet the Lord at any minute. GOD has said for us to be filled with the Spirit (Eph. 5:18). The devil and the carnal mind says that speaking with

tongues and the gifts and manifestations of the Holy
Ghost are not for us today. We can do without the
supernatural power of the Holy Spirit what the early
church demonstrated daily in the might of His
resurrection. We are told, "The Church today is doing
the greater works of Jn. 14:12 through mass media. We
are doing more in our day through radio and television."
No! I thank God for the ministry of radio and television,
but these signs shall still follow a people who believe
(Mark 16:15-20)! If we do not see these things, we do not
believe.

GOD'S PURPOSE IS IN THREE DIMENSIONS

Salvation is progressive. There are three dimensions to
God's salvation. A study of the Scriptures reveals that
God has revealed His purpose in THREES. A key text
for this principle is found in Deut. 16:16 (three feasts).
Then the TABERNACLE OF MOSES is an excellent
example, for it was built in three parts:

THE OUTER COURT	THE HOLY PLACE	THE MOST HOLY PLACE
For all Israel	For the priest	For the High Priest
Jesus (the Saviour)	Christ (the Anointing)	The Lord
Born of the Spirit	Firstfruits of the Spirit	Fullness of Spirit
Born an heir	Earnest of the inheritance	Full possession
Babies	Children	Adults
New birth	Holy Ghost Baptism	Maturity
Little children	Young men	Fathers
Justification	Sanctification	Glorification
Milk	Bread	Meat
Thirty-fold	Sixty-fold	Hundred-fold
Feast of Passover	Feast of Pentecost	Feast of Tabernacles
Baptism in water	Baptism in the Spirit	Baptism in fire
Spirit has been saved	Soul is being saved	Body shall be saved
Common salvation	Great salvation	Eternal salvation
Way	Truth	Life
Dust	Sand	Stars
Faith	Hope	Love
Thanksgiving	Praise	Worship
Prophet	Priest	King
Gentiles	Church	Israel
Walk	Run	Mount up
Natural light	Artificial light	Divine light
Fruit	More fruit	Much fruit
Birthright	Blessing	Inheritance
Jesus the Babe	Jesus the Youth	Jesus the Man
Out of Egypt	Through the wilderness	Into the land

Foolish virgins	Wise virgins	The Watchman
David's first anointing	Second anointing	Third anointing
Gleanings	Harvest	Firstfruits
Divine healing	Divine health	Divine life
Orpah	Naomi	Ruth
Brass vessels	Silver vessels	Gold vessels
Workers	Warriors	Worshippers
Multitudes of disciples	Nine disciples	Peter, James, and John
Little faith	Great faith	All faith
First heaven	Second heaven	Third heaven
Mount Ophel	Mount Moriah	Mount Zion
Remnant of her seed	Sun-clothed Woman	Manchild
Sealed with the circumcision of water baptism	Sealed with the Holy Spirit of promise	Sealed with the Mind of Christ in the forehead

These forty examples are some of the wonderful truths that God wants you and I to know firsthand. So much is ours! Jesus came to redeem us from the curse of the Law (Gal. 3:13). That includes sin, sickness, poverty, and death. The law of the Spirit of life in Christ Jesus has made us free from the law of sin and death (Rom. 8:1-2). Yet two millenniums of tradition have stifled the Church and she has yet to walk in what He died for! There is a sleeping giant in the land. Samson's hair is beginning to grow (Judg. 16:22). Let the WORD be true and every man a liar (Jn. 1:1; Acts 5:29; Rom. 3:4). Somebody is going to renounce the fear and unbelief that grips our land. Somebody is going to arise and walk in the full provision of His redemption!

PRESSING TOWARD THE MARK FOR THE PRIZE OF THE HIGH CALLING

"Brethren, I count not myself to have apprehended; but this one thing I do, forgetting those things which are behind, and reaching forth unto those things which are before, I press toward the mark for the prize of the HIGH CALLING of God in Christ Jesus" (Phil. 3:13-14).

I am not satisfied to be an ordinary Christian. I am not

satisfied with what I am, but I am excited about what I am becoming! I know what it is to taste of the Feast of Passover. I have experienced Jesus the Lamb. I have been born from above. I know that I am a child of God! I have sealed that conversion with water baptism. I am glad that I have experienced the Feast of Pentecost. I am not ashamed of this Gospel or my spiritual heritage. And while arm-chair theologians are discussing it, tens of thousands have been filled with the Holy Ghost! While some debate the reality of the Book of Acts, others have gotten hungry and experienced it! The purpose of Pentecost is to bring us into the Feast of Tabernacles. The heavenly Husbandman will receive the harvest of that third dimension! He will receive the EARLY and the LATTER rain (Js. 5:7). The early or former rain was the outpouring of the Holy Ghost at the former part of this age that you can read about in the Book of Acts. The latter rain is the present visitation at the end of this age that began 81 years ago and is still falling! The latter rain is the HARVEST rain that will bring the harvest to maturity ... He will receive to Himself a glorious and overcoming Church (Eph. 5:25-27). I declare it in the Name of the Lord. There will be some of you who will live to see a visitation of God in your cities that is beyond what you can ask or think.

A new day has dawned. The harvest of the Feast of Tabernacles is at hand. The Lord has begun a world-wide thrust of His Spirit, and He now invites us to be part of that move of God. How will we respond? May we not cut God off by our unbelief. May we not presume that the experience of the new birth is all there is to Christianity. And let us not stop at the Feast of Pentecost. He has delivered us, He is delivering us, and He will yet deliver us. The cloud of God has moved and is moving (Num. 9:15-23). Let us arise to follow that fiery cloud of His glory (Jn. 8:12)!

"And He must needs go through Samaria ... Now

*JACOB'S WELL was there. Jesus... sat thus on
the well: and it was about the SIXTH hour. There
cometh a woman of Samaria to draw water... Jesus
saith unto her, 'Go, call thy husband, and come
hither.' The woman answered and said, 'I have no
husband.' Jesus said unto her, '... thou hast had
FIVE HUSBANDS; and HE whom thou NOW hast
is not thy husband'... The woman then left her
waterpot, and went her way into the city, and saith
to the men, 'Come, see a man, which told me all
things that ever I did: is not this the Christ?' "
(Jn. 4:4,6-7,16-18,28-29).*

We are at the end of the SIXTH hour and beginning of
the SEVENTH. Jesus is the LID to Jacob's well in the
sixth hour. He who is our Propitiation and Mercyseat
(Rom. 3:25) is seated on Jacob's well. There is a Well on
the well. And this WOMAN represents the CHURCH
(Eph. 5:17-33). But this woman is not satisfied, for only
He can satisfy (Psa. 107:9). She has had FIVE husbands.
She has been married to a frustrating experience that
was governed by her FIVE NATURAL SENSES! Some
other names for these husbands are:

1. The living SOUL (1 Cor. 15:44-49).
2. The first man Adam (1 Cor. 15:44-49; Eph.
   4:22).
3. The Jacob nature (Gen. 32:24-32).
4. The Ishmael nature (Gen. 16:1-4).
5. The beast nature (Rev. 13:16-18).
6. The wild ass nature (Deut. 22:10).
7. The Antichrist nature (1 Jn. 2:18-22; 4:1-3).
8. The fleshly mind (Col. 2:18).
9. The natural mind (1 Cor. 2:9-14).
10. The carnal mind (Rom. 8:1-6).

She had lived with a wild beast. Vicious, stubborn,
unyielding. Yet she still comes faithfully each day with

her earthen vessel to draw from that nature. But no
more, for it is approaching the seventh hour. It is noon-
day, when the sun is in its fullest strength. The Sun will
never be any bigger or brighter than it is now. But what
is this? There is a MAN on the well. If she is to draw
from that old nature she will have to move Jesus out of
the way!

The Man on the well will deliver us from the past
frustration of being married to our FIVE natural senses.
He will heal and restore us from the misery of being
yoked together with unbelief (2 Cor. 6:14-18). He will
pour in oil and wine, setting us free from the bondage of
being in union with a walk governed by the:

1. Natural eye (Eccl. 1:8).
2. Natural ear (Acts 17:19-21).
3. Natural feelings (Gen. 27:21-23; Heb. 12:18).
4. Natural tastes (Heb. 2:9).
5. Natural smell (Lev. 21:18).

We have tried those relationships, and they didn't
work. They left us broken, disappointed, and empty.
And so we bring our waterpot again and again, longing
for something ... anything ... that will fill the inner
void.

Our present lover is husband number SIX ... the
number of MAN. We have flirted with the lust of the
flesh, and the lust of the eyes, and the pride of life (1 Jn.
2:15-17). All that is in the world that MAN longs for. All
that is in the world to entice us away from the Man on
the well. All that the world system is trying NOW as it
gropes blindly for satisfaction and purpose and
fulfillment. The SIXTH man is our present lover.

THE MAN ON THE WELL IS THE SEVENTH
MAN! He beckons you to come closer. He is not going to
allow the Woman to draw from Jacob's well any more.
Throw away the old waterpot. Cast it out (Gal. 4:30).
And BECOME the waterpot that will reach into HIM.

HE is the Well and you are the waterpot. And the Well is DEEP (Jn. 4:11; Psa. 42:7). Deep calleth unto deep. Be baptized and immersed into HIM. Plunge into Him Who is your refreshing. He is the sweet water and the living water. Cast your bitternesses of those past relationships into Him and be healed (Ex. 15:23-26)!

Now . . . run into your city and tell everyone that you meet that a new day is come for all men. You are the waterpot now filled with His Life. First a container and now a dispenser of that life! This treasure is in earthen vessels.

Do you really want what the Holy Spirit now speaks to you?

Is it possible that you can partake of what you have heard?

Is there more in God for you than you have ever realized?

The answer to all three questions is YES! All you have to do is drop the old and become the new. Lay aside the weight that so easily besets you and come to the Seventh Man . . . His Name is JESUS. He is the Perfect Man and you are complete in Him . . . only HE can fill the spiritual vacuum in your being. The Seventh Man HAS delivered you, and DOES deliver you, and SHALL deliver you. The Seventh Man is the Overcoming, Risen Lord. The Seventh Man will change your life!

> *"Ho, every one that thirsteth, come ye to the water, and he that hath no money; come ye, buy, and eat . . . Wherefore do ye spend money for that which is not bread? And your labour for that which satisfieth not? . . . Come unto me, all ye that labour and are heavy laden, and I will give you rest. Take my yoke upon you, and learn of me; for I am meek and lowly in heart: and ye shall find rest unto your souls. For my yoke is easy, and my burden is light . . . If any man thirst, let him come unto me, and drink. He that believeth on me . . . out of his*

*belly shall flow rivers of living water...and
everything shall live whither the river
cometh... And the Spirit and the bride say, 'Come.'
And let him that heareth say, 'Come.' And let him
that is athirst come. And whosoever will, let him
take the water of life freely"* (Isa. 55:1-2; Mt.
11:28-30; Jn. 7:37-38; Ezek. 47:9; Rev. 22:17).

III
PRESSING THROUGH TRIBULATION

I believe in the Glorious Church (Eph. 5:27). And a church with His Glory and Nature is an Overcoming Church. Such a people know Jesus as Priest and King. Such a people know that salvation is progressive as well as once-for-all. This people knows that God's promise is not to take a Church out of this world (Jn. 17:15) but to bring His army THROUGH tribulation!

I have been building on a theme: Three Basic Principles for the Overcomer. We must be victorious in our everyday living if the world is to know that Jesus is our Risen Lord. He is your Peace (Eph. 2:14). God wants you to be happy.

> *"Beloved, I wish above all things that thou mayest prosper and be in health, even as thy soul prospereth" (3 John 2).*

> *"My dear friend, I hope everything is going happily with you and that you are as well physically as you are spiritually" (Jerus. Bible).*

This is the reason why I have shared these truths with you. First of all, we must understand that Jesus is Priest AND King. If we only relate to the One Who meets our needs, we will be out of balance. To follow Jesus because of what He DOES for the believer is to follow Jesus in a

carnal way. The essence of sin is the love of self.
Selfishness is sinfulness. The Apostle said that same
thing to the Church at Corinth. Carnality is immaturity.

*"And I, brethren, could not speak unto you as unto
spiritual, but as unto CARNAL, even as unto
BABES in Christ" (1 Cor. 3:1).*

Those who are young in Christ are ever testifying to
the same attitude and actions. Praise Him for His
faithfulness (Phil. 4:19)! But if that is where your
Christianity begins and ends, you are going to be
unhappy. The program of God has more for you.
    The Christian has been programmed with a new
nature. That new nature is God's LOVE. There is a new
dimension of FAITH that operates by a new dimension
of love (Gal. 5:6). Faith is in Christ and Christ is in you.
Love is in Christ and Christ is in you (Col. 1:25-29).
Release the God that is within you!
    Many are not living the overcoming life because they
are self-centered. Their fleshly desires are the focal point
and motivational drive behind their lifestyles. Let us
make the Lord Jesus the Center! The victorious life is
the outflow of HIS Victory! He is our faithful Priest, but
let us go on to know the LORD. Learn to relate to Him as
King. Be balanced. Jesus is Priest and King. I am glad
that you and I can have a balance in our walk with Christ
that will produce His lasting joy! May God deliver us
from our own desires and fill us with His own. May He
help us to lay these foundational truths in our minds as
we become part of a House that will stand (Lk. 6:46-49).
    Our second message dealt with the truth that
salvation is progressive in nature as well as being once-
for-all. We have been saved, we are being saved, and we
shall be saved (2 Cor. 1:10). The philosophy that says,
"Once saved, always saved," does not agree with the
whole of the Scripture. We learned that the word
"salvation" means "COMPLETE DELIVERANCE." It

is an all-inclusive term that embraces the redemption of man's spirit, soul, and body.

We all need more of Jesus. The minute we say that we are completely saved and that there is nothing more to be experienced in the New Covenant is the moment that we begin to spiritually decline. Don't let your religious roots go down so deep that you cannot pull them up and move into present truth (2 Pet. 1:12).

Repentance is a change of mind from that complete state of death in trespasses and sins (Eph. 2:1) to the putting on of the full Mind of Christ (Eph. 4:13). The Greek word for "repentance" is "metanoia" and means "a change of mind." Repentance is not a bad word. The scope of repentance includes the entire change or transformation of your being by the renewing of your mind. This change is from glory to glory (2 Cor. 3:18) and starts at the time when we first repented from sin and received Christ as Saviour.

> "And be not conformed to this world: but be ye transformed by the RENEWING of your MIND, that ye may prove what is that good, and acceptable, and perfect, will of God" (Rom. 12:2).

Repentance is a blessed attitude that every overcomer needs. You and I need to put on a new kind of mind day by day. God is saving our attitudes! There are some ways of thinking that I have that are not spiritual; they are carnal. There are some ways of thinking that you have that are not spiritual; they are carnal.

> "For to be carnally minded is death; but to be spiritually minded is life and peace" (Rom. 8:6).

I bring you good news. We can put on Christ. We can put on more of Jesus. We can think like God and not like men. Let us pray as did Paul:

*"My little children, of whom I travail in birth again
UNTIL Christ be FORMED in you"* (Gal. 4:19).

*"I am in travail with you over again until you take
the shape of Christ"* (New English Bible).

*"I am again suffering birth pangs until Christ is
completely and permanently formed (molded) within
you!"* (Amplified Bible).

*"I am again striving with intense effort and
anguish until Christ be outwardly expressed in
you"* (Wuest's Expanded Translation).

*"Oh, my children, how you are hurting me! I am
once again suffering for you the pains of a mother
waiting for her child to be born—longing for the
time when you will finally be filled with Christ"*
(The Living Bible).

Salvation is progressive. This word for "FORMED" in
Gal. 4:19 is "MORPHOO" and is #3445 in Strong's
Concordance. It means "to fashion, to form (through the
idea of ADJUSTMENT of parts); shape, nature." Wuest
says that this word "refers to the act of giving outward
expression of one's inner nature." Thayer says that this
word speaks of that which is "intrinsic and essential;" in
other words, NATURE. Vine adds that "MORPHOO"
refers "not to the external and transient, but to the
inward and real; it is used in Gal. 4:19, expressing the
necessity of a change in character and conduct to
correspond with inward spiritual condition, so that there
may be moral conformity to Christ." (Compare Mk.
16:12; Phil. 2:6-7.) The Greek word "METAMORPHOO"
is derived from it (Mt. 17:2; Mk. 9:2; Rom. 12:2; 2 Cor.
3:18).

We are being saved. We are being CHANGED. Paul
knew this and prayed for the Galatians. He was praying

for people who already knew Jesus. He was praying for the CHILDREN of God. The Apostle understood that many things had yet to be ADJUSTED in the character and conduct of these believers. This great Body of Christ has many members (1 Cor. 12:12-26). The Holy Ghost is bringing balance and adjustment to the Body of Christ, individually, locally, and universally.

Salvation is the totality of that which God is doing in your life. Thank God for the definite experience of conversion. I know that I am born again. I have been baptized in water to seal that conversion. I know that I am filled with the Holy Ghost. But I also know that God is working in my life on a day-to-day basis. I am being changed:

". . . line upon line, line upon line; here a little, and there a little" (Isa. 28:10).

My blessed hope is not that Jesus will come at any minute. The Man Christ Jesus will come again. He said that He would (Jn. 14:3). That is a fact. I do not have to hope for a fact. But my hope is this:

"See what [an incredible] quality of love the Father has given (shown, bestowed on) us, that we should [be permitted] be named and called and counted the children of God! And so we are! The reason that the world does not know (recognize, acknowledge) us, is that it does not know (recognize, acknowledge) Him. Beloved, we are [even here and] now God's children; it is not yet disclosed (made clear) what we shall be [hereafter], but we know that when He comes and is manifested we shall [as God's children] RESEMBLE AND BE LIKE HIM, for we shall see Him just as He [really] is. And every one who has THIS HOPE [resting] on Him cleanses (purifies) himself just as He is pure—chaste, undefiled, guiltless" (1 Jn. 3:1-3—Amplified Bible).

My hope is to be LIKE Jesus! Chaste, undefiled,
guiltless. There is a people in the earth who are pressing
for the mark for the prize of the high calling of God in
Christ Jesus (Phil. 3:12-14). This people:

> "... are they which were not defiled with women;
> for they are virgins. These are they which follow the
> Lamb whithersoever he goeth. These were redeemed
> from among men, being the firstfruits unto God and
> to the Lamb. And in their mouth was found no guile:
> for they are without fault before the throne of God"
> (Rev. 14:4-5).

Jesus is Priest and King. Salvation is progressive.
These are basic precepts for the overcomer. Now we
come to our third principle: pressing through tribulation.

GIDEON

Many of us are like Gideon. We are cowards. God has
called us to be judges and deliverers. We can certainly
relate to the story of Gideon as recorded in the Book of
Judges, chapters six through eight.

> "... Gideon threshed wheat by the winepress, to
> hide it from the Midianites. And the angel of the
> Lord appeared unto him, and said unto him, The
> Lord is with thee, thou mighty man of
> valour... And he said unto him, Oh my Lord,
> wherewith shall I save Israel? Behold, my family is
> poor in Manasseh, and I am the least in my father's
> house. And the Lord said unto him, Surely I will be
> with thee, and thou shalt smite the Midianites as
> one man" (Judg. 6:11-12,15-16).

Gideon was threshing grain behind the winepress. You
don't thresh grain behind the winepress. You don't

preach this message in a corner (Acts 26:26). You thresh grain in an elevated, open place. We preach this message out in the open where all can see it. Take courage. You are a "mighty man of valour." The Amplified Bible says, "You mighty man of fearless courage!" The coward made his excuses, but God promised an anointing that would smite the enemy as one man. This came to pass in Judg. 7:13 where we read that:

> "... a cake of barley bread tumbled into the host of Midian, and came unto a tent, and smote it that it fell, and overturned it, that the tent lay along ... For we being many are ONE BREAD, and one body: for we are all partakers of that one bread" (1 Cor. 10:17).

Let us rejoice that God is investing His strength and victory in a CORPORATION whose HEAD is the Lord Jesus Christ! The man of faith and power for the hour is the many-membered Body of Christ. But even that is not enough for Gideon. He wants to know for sure that God has spoken. Some of you don't know for sure if you should be bold to proclaim the truths of God. So Gideon threw out a fleece. Be careful. You might get fleeced. Remember that the fleece is mentioned one time in the Bible, and that is here in Judg. 6:36-40 in the Old Testament. But if you insist on throwing out a fleece, then do what Gideon did. Make it doubly impossible!

I have found something better than fleeces. The Word of God as it is energized and brought to life by the power of the Holy Ghost from within. God told Gideon to go home and witness to his family. His father had a grove of idols and Gideon was to destroy it (Judg. 6:25-32). He went at NIGHT with TEN others and obeyed the Lord. The cowardly nature was changed in the act of obedience. Gideon became Jerubaal.

1. Gideon (#1439 in Strong's)—"feller (warrior); to

fell a tree or to destroy anything; cut or hew down."

2. Jerubaal (#3378 in Strong's)—"Baal will
contend; to toss, grapple, to wrangle, hold a
controversy with Baal."

Gideon became a Baal-fighter. Baal was a bull. The
coward became a bullfighter. If you are called to preach
you are called to be a bullfighter. Be encouraged and
understand that:

> "... the weapons of our warfare are not carnal, but
> mighty through God to the pulling down of
> STRONGHOLDS; casting down imaginations, and
> every high thing that exalteth itself..." (2 Cor.
> 10:4-5).

We are called to pull down strongholds. Those
spiritual walled cities and fortresses—the lying vanities,
imaginations, and traditions of the carnal mind. They
are the old teachings that minister death, doubt, and
unbelief. Obey God. Become a bullfighter and tear it
down in the Name of the Lord!

God will not sympathize with our cowardice. He will
expose it so that we will be able to overcome it. God said,
"Gideon, tell everybody that has your problem to go
home."

> "Now therefore go to, proclaim in the ears of the
> people, saying, Whosoever is FEARFUL and
> AFRAID, let him return and depart early from
> mount Gilead. And there returned of the people
> twenty and two thousand; and there remained ten
> thousand" (Judg. 7:3).

History tells us Gideon's 32,000 were already
outnumbered four to one. I believe that the coward
danced and shouted when he discovered that 22,000 of

those other men were just as fearful as he was (1 Cor. 10:13). That encourages me. That comforts me. Be strong in the Lord and in the power of His might (Eph. 6:10).

Gideon's 10,000 became Gideon's 300. They were chosen and separated at the WATER. God will choose His overcomers at the WATER. The water of His WORD! And only those who drink water from the HAND will be chosen for the army of God. I declare to you that there is a living Word in the earth and men called of God to be the voice of the Lord (Eph. 5:26; 4:11). If God has shown you these truths, lift up your voice like a trumpet and spare not (Isa. 58:1).

> *"These are my orders: be firm and brave, never be daunted or dismayed, for the Eternal your God is with you wherever you go" (Josh. 1:9—Moffatt).*

TAKEN OUT OR BROUGHT THROUGH?

We must press through tribulation. We must learn God's methods, plans, and purposes. God's intent is not to take us OUT of pressure, but to lead us and bring us THROUGH pressure. Our lives and ministries must be governed by the clear principles of the Word of God and not by the way that people think.

It is most tempting to teach this third principle from the standpoint of eschatology, or the doctrine of Last Things. I will not cover this truth from the standpoint of Bible prophecy or Jesus' Second Coming. But I will open this concept experimentally and make it most practical. Whether or not we know the truth about Bible prophecy, we need to know how to handle and cope with and overcome the PRESSURE of living in these perilous times! The pressures that we are facing now are greater than anything we have faced heretofore (Josh. 3:4).

We are living in the birth pangs of a new age. We are

experiencing the beginning of sorrows (Matt. 24:5-8).
New kinds of pressures are coming at us in new kinds of
ways. Will we be overwhelmed or will we be overcomers?
This is not a day to walk by sight (2 Cor. 5:7). Those who
are governed by sense knowledge are going to reap the
death of their natural minds. But we are called to walk
after the Spirit. You and I are called to walk after the
Word of God. It is raining on the just and on the unjust
(Matt. 5:45). And the stress and the strain of the old
order gasping for breath and the new order kicking hard
to be born is coming upon the just and the unjust. We
have been caught in a storm. All our rowing is in vain.
All human effort to thwart the stormy wind fulfilling His
Word (Psa. 148:8) is destined to fail. Every social,
political, religious, and technological program of man is
not enough. This is seen most clearly in the Bible
account of Acts 27. God opened that whole chapter to
me several years ago with these four principles:

1. The WIND is the HOLY SPIRIT (Psa. 148:8;
Acts 2:1-4).

2. The STORM is the DAY OF THE LORD (Joel
2:1-2; Zeph. 1:14-18).

3. The SHIP is a WORLD SYSTEM HEADED
FOR THE ROCKS (2 Thess. 1:6-12).

4. And PAUL is an OVERCOMING MAN WHO
WILL TAKE OVER THE SHIP (Eph. 4:13).

This cosmos is an order, a system, an arrangement of
things. It is a lifestyle that is stamped and marked by
the beastly mentality of human genius and the beastly
behaviour of human strength. This world system is
headed for the rocks and ALL of us are on board! All of
us have been caught by a storm from the East
(Euroclydon). All of us are being lashed about with the

fury of God's righteous judgments. What can we do about it? We might as well "let her drive" (Acts 27:15). And we better understand that God is not going to take us out of this storm, but He is going to give us His grace to press through tribulation. There are some "die-hards" on board who are ever trying to escape on the "lifeboat" (Acts 27:16,30-32). But the time will soon come when even that means of escape will be cut off from the minds of God's people.

But why is a storm necessary? The Bible gives us the answer in Psa. 107:23-30 and provides an Old Testament commentary on Acts 27:

> *"They that go down to the sea in SHIPS, that do business in great waters; these see the WORKS of the Lord, and His wonders in the deep. For He commandeth, and raiseth the STORMY WIND, which lifteth up the waves thereof. They mount up to the heaven, they go down again to the depths: their SOUL is melted because of TROUBLE. They reel to and fro, and stagger like a drunken man, and are at their WIT'S END."*

As noted in a previous message, man's SOUL is his intellect, his emotions, and his will. The word for "WIT" in Psa. 107:27 is #2451 in Strong's, and means "wisdom (in mind, word, or act), intelligent, skillful, artful, cunning, subtile." God is bringing an END to man's wisdom, intelligence, and skill. God is moving in your life and mine through pressures to bring an end to our wisdom, intelligence, and skill. We are coming to our wit's end! Hallelujah!

> *"Look upon Zion... there the glorious Lord will be unto us a place of broad rivers and streams; wherein shall go no GALLEY with OARS, neither shall GALLANT ship pass thereby... Thy TACK-LINGS are loosed; they could not well strengthen*

their MAST, they could not spread the SAIL: then is the prey of a great SPOIL divided; the LAME take the prey. And the inhabitant shall not say, I am sick: the people that dwell therein shall be forgiven their iniquity" (Isa. 33:20-24).

Man must be brought to his knees. The margin of Psa. 107:27 says, "all their wisdom swallows itself up." Knox in his translation adds, "all their seamanship forgotten." We have been apprehended for Zion. There are no GALLIES in Zion. There are no SLAVES in Zion who are rowing in their own strength. The GALLANT ships shall not pass by. The PROUD who in leisure and luxury know all the answers and sail into waters of their own choosing are going to be broken in the Day of the Lord. Has God loosened your tacklings? Has He dealt with your mast so that you cannot spread your sail? The SAIL speaks of that which gives energy and strength to the DIRECTION of a ship, and the tacklings and the mast SUPPORT the sail. I am simply saying that you and I are under the dealings of the Lord and we cannot CHART OUR *OWN* COURSE! This is for our GOOD, for the Father desires to divide the great spoil of Jesus' victory and only the LAME can receive it. God must smite our human strength. Jacob's thigh has to be dealt with (Gen. 32:24-32). Only those who have met God face to face in the night season can partake of the inheritance. Only those who have pressed through a stormy wind will take the prey. There must be a battle if there is to be a victory. I must lose my life to obtain His life. There is an overcoming Church on the horizon who will be forgiven of all iniquity and healed of all diseases (Psa. 103:3). We must decrease that the Christ in us can increase and come forth in victory. God loves us. He wants to help us. This storm is of God. Some have been taught otherwise, and so they cry,

"Oh, that I had wings like a dove! For then would I

fly away and be at rest... I would hasten my escape from the WINDY STORM and tempest" *(Psa. 55:6,8).*

THE SOURCE OF PRESSURE: GOD OR THE DEVIL?

Too many today have done what Paul said not to do:

"Neither give place to the devil" (Eph. 4:27).

"And give no opportunity to the Devil" (Twentieth Century N.T.)

"You must not give the devil a chance" (Goodspeed).

"Don't give the devil that sort of foothold" (Phillips).

"Leave no loop-hole for the devil" (New English Bible).

"And stop giving an occasion for acting [opportunity] to the devil" (Wuest's Expanded Translation).

"Leave no [such] room or foothold for the devil—give no opportunity to him" (The Amplified Bible).

Everything negative that comes your way is not of the devil. Most people are double-minded (Jas. 6:8). Most people have a mind that operates by the principle of DUALITY and not SINGLENESS. Their frame of mind sees God AND the devil, and, from a practical observation, the devil is just as big if not bigger than

God. To these who see the negative above the positive, the devil is big, and mean, and nasty. I believe in a DEFEATED devil (Matt. 12:25-30; Acts 2:24; Rom. 8:37; 1 Cor. 5:5; 2 Cor. 2:14; Matt. 16:18; Mk. 16:15-20; Acts 26:15-19; Eph. 1:18-23; 6:16; Col. 1:9-14; 2:15; Heb. 2:14-15; 1 Pet. 2:24; 1 Jn. 3:8)!

People often attribute certain things to the devil and unwittingly do that which he wants: worship him. Satan is a dog on a leash. He is being used of the Father (Job 1:6-12; 2:1-6). That which took place in Job's life was initiated by GOD and not Satan (Job 1:8). Jesus has bound the strong man, so let me encourage you to go down to the gates of hell and get some building material so we can get God's House ready so that Jesus can come to live in it! That Body of Christ that HE is building is going to be an overcoming people who are going to stand in the evil day.

Do you understand the source or the purpose of pressure? GOD will bring a lot your way to CROSS the way that you think, the way that you feel, and the way that you want. Your soul and your carnal mind will be crossed by the Lord. GOD'S positive becomes YOUR negative. And some teach that ANYTHING negative that comes your way is not of the Lord, but of the devil. We are not ignorant of Satan's devices (2 Cor. 2:11). Put on Christ and stand your ground (Eph. 6:13-14). But I beseech you to be balanced and realize that:

> "... the desires of the flesh are opposed to the (Holy) Spirit, and the [desires of the] Spirit are opposed to the flesh (Godless human nature); for these are antagonistic to each other—continually withstanding and in conflict with each other—so that you are not free but are prevented from doing what you desire to do" (Gal. 5:17—Amplified Bible).

The King James Version says that the flesh and Spirit are "contrary." This word is the Greek word

"ANTIKEIMAI" (#480 in Strong's) and means "to lie opposite; be adverse (repugnant) to; adversary, be contrary, oppose." Thayer adds, "to be set over against, to withstand." There is a verse in the Old Testament that clarifies these truths:

> "But they rebelled, and vexed his holy Spirit: therefore he was turned to be their ENEMY, and he fought against them" (Isa. 63:10).

> "But they, they thwarted him, they pained his sacred Spirit; and so he turned to be their foe, he fought himself against them" (Moffatt).

> "But they rebelled, they grieved his holy spirit. Then he turned enemy, and himself waged war on them" (Jerusalem Bible).

Everything that happened to Israel in the Old Testament happened for our example and learning (1 Cor. 10:11; Rom. 15:4). When Israel rebelled against the Lord, he became their ENEMY! God becomes your enemy when you walk after the flesh, for the carnal mind is HOSTILE toward God (Rom. 8:7).

Now look at those verses in Isaiah 63 that precede verse 10:

> "I will mention the lovingkindnesses of the Lord, and the praises of the Lord, according to all that the Lord hath bestowed on us, and the great goodness toward the house of Israel, which He hath bestowed on them according to His mercies, and according to the multitude of His lovingkindnesses. For He said, Surely they are My people, children that will not lie: so He was their Saviour. In all their AFFLICTION He was afflicted, and the angel of His presence saved them: in His love and in His pity He redeemed them; and He bare them, and carried them all the days of old" (Isa. 63:7-9).

He was their Saviour in all their AFFLICTIONS. We have a High Priest who can be touched with the feelings of our infirmities (Heb. 4:15). He has sat where we sit (Ezek. 3:15). But God's people, then and now, rebel and grieve the Holy Ghost. Then God becomes your adversary. Whenever the believer frustrates the grace of God by being bull-headed in his conceit, or stubbornness, or pride, or bitterness, or resentment, the HOLY Spirit becomes his enemy. In that moment the Holy Ghost becomes the adversary against that UNHOLY attitude. And for our GOOD, God will fight with us . . . to correct us. God will train and discipline us as sons. This will produce the peaceable fruit of righteousness in us (Heb. 12:5-11). To be carnally minded is death. God wants us to live. God will trouble us, and we will learn to press through this tribulation.

EVERYTHING NEGATIVE THAT HAPPENS IN YOUR LIFE IS NOT THE DEVIL

It is most important in this hour that we be balanced in our preaching and our practice. Everything negative that happens in your life is not of the devil. Some of it is. But there are many practical areas of our lives in the home and the local church that need to be addressed in the light of these principles.

There are those who presume to have a ministry. There is a classic example of this in the Old Testament:

"Then said Ahimaaz the son of Zadok, Let me now run, and bear the king tidings . . . And Joab said unto him, Thou shalt not bear tidings this day, but thou shalt bear tidings another day . . . Then said Joab to Cushi, Go tell the king what thou hast seen. And Cushi bowed himself unto Joab, and ran. Then said Ahimaaz the son of Zadok YET AGAIN to Joab, But howsoever, let me, I pray thee, also run

> *after Cushi. And Joab said, Wherefore wilt thou run,*
> *my son, seeing that THOU HAST NO TIDINGS*
> *READY? But howsoever, said he, let me run. And*
> *he said unto him, Run . . .And the king said, Is the*
> *young man Absalom safe? And Ahimaaz*
> *answered . . . I saw a great tumult, but I KNEW*
> *NOT WHAT IT WAS. And the king said unto him,*
> *Turn aside, and stand here. And he turned aside,*
> *and stood still" (2 Sam. 18:19-23,29-30).*

Ahimaaz means "brother of anger." The angry young
man had never learned of the basic principles of God's
Kingdom. He was impulsive and self-willed. Even with
his stubborn attitudes, he knows that something is
happening. He is a "good man" (verse 27) but that is not
enough. Unlike Cushi, he has never bowed in submission
to older warriors. Hear him cry, "Let me now preach!"
So many today have "no tidings of any profit" (Verse
22—Rotherham). The revelation has never been birthed
in their spirit or worked out through tribulation. They
are not proven. Young preacher, have you identified with
a local assembly? Have you been trained by older
ministry? Do you know what God is saying today? An
immature ministry will fall apart. People are hurt and
the devil is blamed. Nonsense! Stop blaming the devil for
the problems caused by man's rebellion! We are going to
reap what we sow. Some preachers are running without a
message. Some singers are worse as they presume that
the yoke shall be destroyed through talent (Isa. 10:27).
Then every problem and setback is blamed on the devil.
Have you ever considered that the Lord is trying to shut
down YOUR program that you might stand still long
enough to be part of HIS program? These are not
suffering for righteousness' sake (Mt. 5:10). But Peter
explained what is happening: you might be suffering as a
fool.

> *"But let none of you suffer as a murderer, or as a*

thief, or as an evildoer, or as a busybody in other men's matters" (1 Pet. 4:15).

"... or as a mischief-maker (a meddler) in the affairs of others—infringing on their rights" (The Amplified Bible).

"... or a bad character or a revolutionary" (Moffatt).

"... or as a self-appointed overseer in other men's matters" (Wuest).

"... or as an inspector into other men's matters" (Young's Literal).

"... or making trouble or being a busybody and prying into other people's affairs" (The Living Bible).

I challenge you to take a real good look at your life or ministry. Everything that is in the realm of the negative cannot be wrapped in one blanket statement and given to the devil. As a pastor, I know that sheep get themselves into trouble because of their own stubbornness. They do not want to face the root of their heartache: their own rebellion.

Abraham produced Ishmael with a good idea and faith in a good idea, and Ishmael was a WILD man (Gen. 16:1-4,12). He was a wild ass, untamed and fierce. That same nature in us will reproduce itself in our own ambitions and desires. We will always give birth to that which is within ourselves. It will look like us. It will BE us! God is going to deal with you and me face to face and then cast out every wild thing that we have produced (Gen. 17:18; 21:9-14). GOD is troubling you, Abraham, to produce a Divine nature in you that will multiply itself into a nation!

I PRAY NOT THAT THOU SHOULDEST
TAKE THEM OUT OF THE WORLD

God wants to lead us through pressure. "Trouble" or "tribulation" are not always bad words. There are times when God will bring tribulation to our ways that His purposes might be accomplished in us. You that are parents know this is true. You bring tribulation to your children every time you cross their way. You that are pastors know this is true. You bring tribulation into your church every time you preach the truth that crosses the way that the sheep want to go (Prov. 22:15; Isa. 53:6). The children in the home and the saints in the church must grow up. They must press through tribulation.

Jesus Christ ever liveth to make intercession for us (Rom. 8:34; Heb. 7:25). He is at the right hand of the Father. Some only recognize His ministry in the past but fail to realize that He is still ministering in our behalf. There are three appearings of Jesus:

1. HE *HAS* APPEARED (Heb. 9:26)—the High Priest at the Brazen Altar.

2. HE *NOW* APPEARS (Heb. 9:24)—the High Priest beyond the Veil.

3. HE *SHALL* APPEAR (Heb. 9:28)—the High Priest revealing Himself to all.

On the Day of Atonement (Lev. 16), the High Priest appeared at the Brazen Altar with the blood. Jesus Christ HAS appeared on Calvary's cross to put away sin by the sacrifice of Himself by the shedding of His own blood. Then the High Priest took the blood beyond the Veil to bring the nation of Israel into the Presence of God. Jesus Christ NOW appears in the Presence of God for us, bearing us up on His shoulders, and strapped to

His heart of love! After sin had been fully atoned for, the High Priest then returned to the people and revealed himself to the nation. Jesus Christ SHALL appear without sin unto salvation and every eye shall see Him. Having fully put away and dealt with sin in the lives of a perfected people, He shall literally appear. He HAS appeared, and He NOW appears, and He SHALL appear!

The majority of the Church world wants to escape from their problems, and they are praying accordingly. Is it possible that we could be asking amiss (Jas. 4:3)? We must do everything in the Name or NATURE of the Lord Jesus (Col. 3:17). We must pray as HE prayed. We must pray as HE now prays. If we are to walk with Him, we must then AGREE with Him (Amos 3:3) and His prayer life! But how is He praying?

Jesus is our great High Priest and now appears in the Presence of God for us. His High Priestly prayer is given to us in John 17:1-26. I believe that those who are called to be Christians are to be LIKE the Lord in their praying. I believe in prayer, and I believe that this prayer in John 17 is still pouring forth from His heart! This Scripture gives us some real insight into the High Priestly prayer life of the Lord. And what did He say? And what is He saying?

> *"I pray NOT that thou shouldest take them out of the world, but that thou shouldest keep them from the evil" (Jn. 17:15).*

> *"I do not ask that Thou wilt remove them out of the world, but that Thou wilt protect them from the Evil One" (Weymouth).*

> *". . . but that you should guard them safely from the reach of the Pernicious One" (Wuest's Expanded Translation).*

"I'm not asking you to take them out of the world, but to keep them safe from Satan's power" (The Living Bible).

"I do not ask that Thou mayest take them out of the world, but that Thou mayest keep them out of the evil" (Young's Literal).

It is obvious that we could teach this message from the standpoint of the Second Coming of Jesus, (Prov. 10:30) but we want to remain practical. Let me give a few more examples of what it means to press through tribulation.

Have you met the kind of person who can never keep a steady job? The first day that something goes wrong, they want to quit and look for another job. And usually the thing that went wrong was that the boss expected his money's worth! They might complain about the working conditions, but most folk simply want to complain about work. The carnal mind is lazy. It doesn't want to work or exert itself. It is ever asking, "What do I have to do?" Then there are those who somehow and somewhere got the notion that a preacher can't walk by faith and still have a job. Beloved, let's have some balance!

Have you met the "professional student?" This is the kind of person who still thinks that he is in high school. This young person goes to college and discovers a different world . . . a real one. He meets some teachers who don't give out A's and B's like lollipops. He will have to work and study if he is going to make it. "Well, I think I'll try another college. I don't like this one."

And have you met the kind of Christian that is unstable as water (Gen. 49:4)? I have met so many who have no spiritual roots. They say, "Well, I think I'll try another church. I don't like this one." Folks go looking for the church of their own choice. People are looking for a place, or a job, or a college, or a church where there are no adversities, or problems, or anything that crosses or inconveniences them. In the Church realm, some of these folk eventually meet a ministry and a message that projects the Lordship of Jesus Christ. This Gospel of the Kingdom declares His Kingship in such a way that folks will have to submit to the will and the Word of God. They will have to change those unholy attitudes of immaturity and escapism. If they refuse to change they leave. When something goes against your will what do you do? Do you avoid pain, suffering and growing up in God or do you want to be taken out of the world? Are you pressing through tribulation?

THE TIME OF JACOB'S TROUBLE

Every one of you sometime in life will experience the tribulation of facing the truth of who and what you are. Every one of us will have an experience like Jacob had. There was a time of Jacob's trouble (Jer. 30:7). I will again lay aside my prophetical aspects of this verse and look to the experimental and the practical. I know that Jacob went through *his* tribulation the night that he met God face to face!

"And Jacob was left ALONE; and a Man wrestled with him until daybreak. And when [the Man] saw that He did not prevail against [Jacob], He touched the hollow of his thigh; and Jacob's thigh was out of joint as he wrestled with Him. Then He said, Let me go, for day is breaking. But Jacob said, I will not let You go unless You declare a blessing upon me. [The Man] asked him, What is your name? And [in SHOCK of REALIZATION, WHISPERING] he said, Jacob—SUPPLANTER, SCHEMER, TRICK-STER, SWINDLER! And he said, Your name shall be called no more Jacob [supplanter], but Israel [contender with God]; for you have contended and

have power with God and with men, and have
PREVAILED ... And Jacob called the name of the
place Peniel [the face of God], saying, For I have
seen God FACE TO FACE ... And as he passed
Penuel [Peniel] the sun rose upon him, and he was
limping because of his thigh" (Gen. 32:24-32—
Amplified Bible).

Jacob had run from God for 20 years. But God caught
up with him. And Jacob was left ALONE. No crowds.
No noise. No Mom. No Dad. No pastor. Just you and
God! We are going to meet God face to face and confess
our name (NATURE). God is going to trouble us until
the BREAKING. And the DAYSTAR is going to arise
out of the night seasons to reveal the Israel, or Christ
nature (2 Pet. 1:19). God is going to "TOUCH" us. This
word is #5060 in Strong's and means "to touch, to lay
the HAND upon (Eph. 4:11), to reach, to strike violently,
beat, plague, or smite." This is more than just a love-tap.
Consider these examples:

1. "Surely he hath borne our griefs, and carried our
sorrows: yet we did esteem him STRICKEN,
smitten of God, and afflicted" (Isa. 53:4).

2. "... STRIKE the lintel and the two side posts
with the blood that is in the basin ..." (Ex. 12:22).

3. "And Azariah the chief priest, and all the priests,
looked upon him, [King Uzziah of Judah] and,
behold, he was leprous in his forehead, and they
thrust him out from thence; yea, himself hasted also
to go out, because the Lord had SMITTEN him" (2
Chron. 26:20).

4. "And, behold, there came a great wind from the
wilderness, and SMOTE the four corners of the
house, and it fell ..." (Job 1:19).

In the time of Jacob's trouble, he was smitten by the Lord. And the Jacob nature in us will have to be smitten by the Lord. There is a Christ or an Israel nature that God wants to come forth in each of us. He wants us to be PREVAILERS. God wants us to be OVERCOMERS. "PREVAILED" is #3201 in Strong's and means "to be able; attain, endure, might, overcome, have power." This new nature will display itself when our THIGH is smitten. The thigh speaks of our STRENGTH, and especially our strength to REPRODUCE or CREATE. Our ability to bring forth must decrease that His ability to bring forth in us might increase (Jn. 3:30). Have you met God? Has He touched you? If there is any desire in you at all for Him and His Kingdom, let me assure you that you will encounter Him in this dimension. Those who are Israelites indeed (Jn. 1:47) are betrayed by the way that they WALK! There is a familiar limp in their life and ministry that reveals the Lord. They are not so quick on the trigger. They have learned to wait upon the Lord. The Sun has arisen upon them and they walk in the light of His countenance.

I would rather go into the Kingdom maimed than not go in at all. I would rather that the Lord cripple my desires and be the Good Shepherd who in love does break my spiritual legs than to miss God altogether. There is a nature in us that must be dealt with. Every man and woman must face this. If you long for Him, then know that He must change your name. The Lord Jesus wants to deliver us from hypocrisy and bring us into the reality of the overcoming life. He wants us to have power with God and men. He wants us to prevail.

"GET ME OUT OF THIS LIONS' DEN!"

This is the Year of Jubilee. This is a time of great release and deliverance! There has never been a day like this day before (Lev. 25; Lk. 4:18). But God's ways are not like our ways. His methods differ from the natural mind. Like Daniel the prophet, we must experience the lions' den. And the den of lions is ordained of the Lord to deal with the den of thieves. Jesus said,

> "My HOUSE shall be called the HOUSE OF PRAYER, but ye have made it a DEN OF THIEVES" (Matt. 21:13).

Is your life a house of prayer or a den of thieves? Am I building God a house of devotion or am I scheming to climb in some other way (Jn. 10:1)? Daniel prayed his way into the lions' den. But most of us want to pray our way OUT of the lions' den (Dan. 6:1-28)! The carnal mind wants to flee from the lion, but listen to these words of the prophet Amos:

> "Woe unto you that desire the Day of the Lord! To what end is it for you? The day of the Lord is darkness and not light. As if a man did FLEE FROM A LION, and a BEAR met him; or went into the house, and leaned his hand on the wall, and a SERPENT bit him" (Amos 5:18-19).

There is no escape. In the day of His anger, are you going to be in the Ark or trying to get in? We want to avoid the lions' den. David knew nothing of the giant when he killed the lion and the bear (1 Sam. 17:37). To those who are after God's heart, let me exhort you: "DAVID, YOU'VE GOT A GOLIATH AHEAD OF YOU!!" Goliath was death in action. You're sent to overcome it. The lion and the bear experience is a God-ordained taskmaster for a greater victory. Do not flee the lion. Your deliverance is right where your problem is.

The lions' den was a blessing. It made the king fast and pray! No manner of hurt will come upon you, because you believe in your God. The night season with the lions will bring the enemies of God and their companions to nought. Kings will then decree to the nations the greatness of our God and prophesy of the majesty of His Kingdom! And Daniel prospered (Dan. 6:28).

May God help us to look at things from His perspective. He is working out His purposes in us as we submit to His ways. There is a glorious Church on the horizon that knows that the trial of our faith is much more precious than gold that perisheth (1 Pet. 1:7) and that we must press through tribulation into the fullness of our Living Head (Eph. 4:15).

These principles are desperately needed to balance what we have heard concerning faith and prosperity. God does not want His people to be snared by extremes or tangents. We must be balanced, declaring the whole Word of God.

WE WERE PICKED OUT TO BE PICKED ON

Contrary to popular opinion, we did not decide to follow Jesus. He Who is the True Vine declared,

> *"Ye have NOT chosen me, but I HAVE CHOSEN YOU, and ordained you, that ye should go and bring forth fruit, and that your fruit should remain" (Jn. 15:16).*

> *"It was not you that picked me out, but I picked out you" (Rieu).*

> *"You did not make me the object of your choice for yourselves, but I selected you out for myself" (Wuest's Expanded Translation).*

Jesus loved to break traditions. He did so here, for it was the custom of the Jews that a disciple could choose his own master. Paul the Apostle knew of this, for he said:

"Blessed be the God and Father of our Lord Jesus Christ, who hath blessed us with every spiritual blessing in the heavenlies in Christ, according as HE MADE CHOICE OF US in Him before the founding of the world, that we might be holy and blameless in His presence; in love MARKING US OUT BEFOREHAND unto sonship, through Jesus Christ, for Himself, according to the good pleasure of HIS will..." (Eph. 1:3-5—Rotherham).

We have been picked out to be picked on. The man who has no experiential understanding of the Father's dealings with his sons is a man who will never be an overcomer. In our affliction, we will seek Him early (Hos. 5:15). God deals with us as SONS.

"And have you [completely] forgotten the divine word of appeal and encouragement in which you are reasoned with and addressed as SONS? My son, do not think lightly or scorn to submit to the CORRECTION and DISCIPLINE of the Lord, nor lose courage and give up and faint when you are REPROVED or corrected by Him; for the Lord corrects and disciplines every one whom He loves, and He punishes, even scourges, every son whom He accepts and welcomes to His heart and cherishes... but He disciplines us for our certain good, that we may become sharers in His own holiness. For the time being no discipline brings joy but seems grievous and painful, but afterwards it yields peaceable FRUIT of RIGHTEOUSNESS to those who have been trained by it" (Heb. 12:5-6,10-11—The Amplified Bible).

If somebody is always picking on you, praise the Lord! Maintain this attitude: "Go ahead and pick on me... I am a tree full of fruit. Go ahead, that's why I grew it!"
Those who do not know the ways of the Father often

become bitter and angry. Do you remember the story of Paul and Silas recorded in Acts 16? They were led by the Spirit to the Roman province of Macedonia to preach the Gospel. Although a Roman citizen, Paul was beaten and thrown into the "inner prison." This room might well have been the bottom cell which would have received the waste of the prison. They were thrown into the sewer and had a LEGAL right to complain, but they praised God who led them there! Start singing unto the Lord. The other prisoners are listening. There would have been no release for the others if Paul and Silas had not suffered for righteousness' sake.

KEPT DURING THE HOUR OF TRIAL

God will keep us during the hour of trial. There are many Scriptures to substantiate this truth. One of the most important passages is Exodus 7-12. Just as the plagues came upon Egypt, so our nation and the world system is being judged. Listen to the prophet Jeremiah:

> *"Once Babylon was a golden cup, that made the whole world drunk; the NATIONS drank her wine, and lay before her helpless. Suddenly Babylon falls and breaks! Wail for the creature? Get balsam for her wounds—perhaps she can be cured? 'No,' you answer, 'we would fain have healed her, but there is no curing Babylon; we must leave her to her fate, and all go home, for her doom rises up to heaven..."* (Jer. 51:7-9—Moffatt).

The Authorized Version says, "Therefore the nations are MAD." This word in Strong's Concordance is #1984 and can be rendered as "to be (clamourously) foolish, to rave, rage;" Wilson, in his Old Testament Word Studies, adds, "to be puffed up in vain glory, to vaunt, to rave with foolish conceit; madness implies so great a departure from wisdom that the mind, without any control, rushes on with blind fury." (Compare 1 Sam. 21:13; Psa. 102:8; Eccl. 2:2; 7:7; Isa. 44:25; Jer. 25:16; 50:38.)

The world system is rushing on in blind fury. The nations are mad. Pharaoh's days are numbered. There are no answers. Mankind is at its wit's end. Every bit of human wisdom and genius will find no solution. There can be no peace apart from the Prince of Peace!

We have written a book entitled, "A Lamb for a House." Contained in that message is a detailed account of God's keeping power. The messenger of death is passing through the nation. Homes are being ripped asunder. The blood of the Passover Lamb is our only hope.

Under the leadership of Moses, the Old Testament nation learned to endure in times of trouble. We must come into a living experience of knowing the Lord Who is the Keeper of the pavilion. We must walk in the reality of the secret of His Presence and His tabernacle. God's people must walk with Jesus Christ in such reality that they KNOW He is a God Who will take care of them and meet their needs supernaturally.

I am alarmed at the number of Christians who have never trusted God to meet the needs of their lives. So many are lacking in the exercise of their faith, and have become soft, pampered and lukewarm (Rev. 3:16). They want nothing to do with the thought of hardship or tribulation. God has a people who know by experience that God keeps us in the hour of trial (Dan. 11:32).

Society is crumbling. Babylon is crumbling. This world system is headed for the rocks (Acts 27). When God judged Egypt, He preserved His people!

> *"And I will SEVER in that day the land of Goshen, in which MY PEOPLE dwell, that no swarms of flies shall be there; to the end thou mayest know that I am the Lord in the MIDST of the earth. And I*

*will put a DIVISION between MY PEOPLE and
thy people: tomorrow shall this sign be ... And the
Lord shall SEVER between the cattle of Israel and
the cattle of Egypt ... Only in the land of Goshen,
where the CHILDREN OF ISRAEL were, was
there NO hail ... They saw not one another, neither
rose any from his place for three days: but all the
CHILDREN OF ISRAEL had LIGHT in their
dwellings ... and when I see the BLOOD, I will
PASS OVER you" (Ex. 8:22-23; 9:4,26; 10:23; 12:13).*

The word for "SEVER" (#6395) means "to
distinguish; put a difference, separate, set apart;" the
Theological Wordbook of the Old Testament adds, "to
be distinct, or marked out, discriminate, a certain one."
Wilson in his Word Studies adds, "to separate in a
distinguishing, marvelous manner."

The word for "DIVISION" (#6304) means
"distinction, deliverance; division, redeem, redemption."
It is derived from #6929 ("precedence") and #6923 ("to
project, precede; to anticipate, hasten, meet [usually for
help], prevent").

God makes a difference. He hastens to meet the needs
of His people. God keeps His children during the hour of
trial. In the church world right now, God is separating
the sheep from the goats. It is harvest time and He is
dividing (Matt. 13:37-43). Jesus Christ, our Kinsman-
Redeemer, our Heavenly Boaz, is down at the
threshing-floor dividing His harvest (Ruth 3:2). At this
time, He is threshing the FIRSTFRUITS of the harvest.
God is sanctifying and protecting His own.

*"Know ye that the Lord He is God: it is He that hath
made us, and not we ourselves; we are His people,
and the SHEEP of His pasture ... The Lord is my
shepherd; I shall not want" (Psa. 100:4; 23:1).*

THE WAY OF THE WILDERNESS

I challenge you to look into the Book. Jesus is a Priest and King. This walk is progressive. God wants to take you through the pressure. Now let's look at some more Scripture:

> *"And it came to pass, when Pharaoh had let the people go, that God led them NOT through the way of the land of the Philistines, although that was near... But God LED the people about, THROUGH the way of the WILDERNESS of the Red Sea: and the children of Israel went up HARNESSED out of the land of Egypt" (Ex. 13:17-18).*

This is a day of instant things. We can walk into a room and get instant light by flipping a button. We get up in the morning and drink instant coffee and eat instant grits. God doesn't believe in "short cuts." But Israel had not yet been proven. They were not ready for warfare. We must see the love of God in leading Israel through the wilderness. Are you glad that He will take you through? There are those who cry to be delivered from God's plan of salvation. But when you run from a problem, you take it to the other side of the fence, because the problem is internal. I'll guarantee you that we can't take it into the Kingdom (1 Cor. 6:9-11).

God led His people THROUGH the way of the wilderness. The Word says that:

> *"... JESUS [was] LED up of the SPIRIT into the WILDERNESS, to be tempted of the devil... For as many as are LED by the Spirit of God, they are the sons of God" (Matt. 4:1; Rom. 8:14).*

There is an "ARE LED" company. Not used to be led, or want to be led, but "ARE LED." He that hath an ear,

let him hear. Those who are hearing the voice of God's
Spirit in this hour are being brought through.

"And the children of Israel went up HARNESSED
out of the land of Egypt." This word is #2571 and means
"staunch; to be stout." It is also rendered as "in battle
array" or "by five in a rank" or "by fifties." At first
glance, that seems to be a good thing, but a closer look
will reveal that this baby nation had a mind of its own.
When we are first delivered from the bondage of sin, we
want to go out and conquer the world. It takes a while to
learn that the battle is the Lord's. This verse in Ex.
13:17 also says,

> *"Lest peradventure the people repent when they see
> war, and they return to Egypt."*

Can you picture this homemade army? They were
doing the best that they knew. I can hear them now.
"Let's get this thing organized, Moses." But you cannot
turn a slave into a soldier overnight. In a time of
pressure, the slave nature will come forth.

> *"And when Pharaoh drew nigh, the children of
> Israel lifted up their eyes, and behold, the
> Egyptians marched after them; and they were sore
> AFRAID: and the children of Israel cried out unto
> the Lord. And they said unto Moses, 'Because there
> were no graves in Egypt, hast thou taken us away
> to die in the wilderness?'... And Moses said unto
> the people, 'Fear ye not,... The Lord shall FIGHT
> for you, and ye shall hold your peace'"* (Ex.
> 14:10-14).

The battle array had disintegrated into chaos. Those
who had been harnessed in their homemade armor were
now harnessed by their own fears. We must understand
that just because we have been saved or born again does
not mean we have come into complete liberty. We have

been brought up out of Egypt, but Egypt has not been brought up out of us. Do you remember the raising of Lazarus?

> *"And he that was DEAD came forth, BOUND hand and foot with GRAVECLOTHES: and his face was BOUND about with a napkin. Jesus saith unto them, 'Loose him, and let him go'... And you hath He quickened, who were DEAD in trespasses and sins" (Jn. 11:44; Eph. 2:1).*

There are many things about us that are still harnessed and shackled and bound. The story of Lazarus is a beautiful picture of what I am saying. Praise God that we have been raised from the death of trespasses and sins! But did you know that we came forth from that experience bound from head to foot? There must be a further word from the Holy Ghost that says: "Loose him and let him go!" It is not enough to be born again. You must be loosed! We need to be released in our minds, works, and walk. We need liberty in our seeing, hearing, and speaking.

ALL THAT HAS HAPPENED
AND ALL THAT HAS BEEN WRITTEN

> *"Moreover, brethren, I would not that ye should be ignorant, how that all our fathers were under the cloud, and all passed through the sea; and were all baptized unto Moses in the cloud and in the sea; and did all eat the same spiritual meat; and did all drink the same spiritual drink: for they drank of that spiritual Rock that followed them: and that Rock was Christ... Now all these things HAPPENED unto them for ensamples: and they are WRITTEN for our admonition, upon whom the ends of the world are come... For whatsoever things were*

*WRITTEN aforetime were written for our learning,
that we through patience and comfort of the
scriptures might have hope... And beginning at
Moses and all the prophets, he [Jesus] expounded
unto them in all the scriptures the things
concerning himself" (1 Cor. 10:1-4,11; Rom. 15:4; Lk.
24:27).*

All that has happened and all that has been written is
for US! All Scripture is God-breathed and profitable (2
Tim. 3:16). The Lord Jesus revealed Himself from the
law of Moses, the prophets and the psalms (Lk. 24:44).

We have been brought out of Egypt by the blood of the
Passover Lamb (Jn. 1:29), but we are still harnessed. We
need the wilderness to help us to grow up. The
wilderness in the Bible speaks of discipline, testing, trial,
pressure, purification. Stop kicking against the very
thing that God has provided to set you free. God knows
what He is doing.

*"And thou shalt remember all the way which the
Lord thy God LED thee these forty years in the
WILDERNESS, to HUMBLE thee, and to PROVE
thee, to know what was in thine heart, whether thou
wouldest keep His commandments, or no" (Deut.
8:2).*

*"... to teach you your need of Him, to prove you, to
find out if it was your purpose to obey His orders or
not" (Moffatt).*

*"... to test you and know your inmost heart..."
(Jerusalem Bible).*

*"... humbling you and testing you to find out how
you would respond, and whether or not you would
really obey Him?" (Living Bible).*

"To know" could be rendered as "to get to know." God wanted to get to know His people. But beyond that, He wanted His people to get to know themselves and the God that was leading them. Jehovah already knew the hearts of His people. He knows your heart and mine. But God wants us to know even as we are known (1 Cor. 13:12). God wants us to be as confident in the One who is in us as He is. We are maturing in our knowledge of the Son who is within us (Eph. 4:13; Gal. 4:6). The Father knows what we are becoming. He sees the end from the beginning. He wants us to see and to know ourselves as HE sees and knows us. The wilderness is necessary. There are no options or shortcuts. We will never know how strong we are in God until we have been proven.

THE FAITH AND PROSPERITY MESSAGE

Much has been said across the Body of Christ in the last fifteen years concerning our position in Christ and the need of speaking it into being. You are what you say you are. This is true. The first three chapters of Ephesians deals with the WEALTH of the believer. We need to know that. But we also need to know about those last three chapters of Ephesians that reveal the WALK and the WARFARE of the believer. We must be balanced.

> "Beloved, I wish above all things that thou mayest prosper and be in health, EVEN AS thy soul prospereth" (3 Jn. 2).

God wants us to prosper. God wants us to be in health. I believe that and I preach that and I practice that. But God also wants us to press through tribulation! You and I must be discerning and get a solid, balanced perspective of God's plan for our lives, or we are going to miss the very thing that can save us.

There has been a subtle principle creeping through the
body of Christ that says that ANYTHING negative or
adverse is wrong. God sent Israel into an environment of
adversity. We have dealt with this dimension of the
carnal mind throughout this manuscript, so we do not
need to repeat it at length. But we must have a balanced
diet of spiritual things. I am going to preach a balanced
Word. I want my children to eat a balanced diet and
grow up to be strong and healthy. And I want you to
grow up to be strong and healthy in Jesus. And Jesus
will take you through!

> *"And when we departed from Horeb, we went
> THROUGH all that GREAT and TERRIBLE
> wilderness, which ye saw by the way of the
> mountain of the Amorites, as the Lord our God
> commanded us; and we came to Kadesh-barnea"
> (Deut. 1:19).*

Note that God's people are still going THROUGH. I
am talking about balance. We must understand that the
wilderness is GREAT. And we must understand that the
wilderness is TERRIBLE.

Did you ever learn to eat spinach? I am talking about
those things that don't taste so good but which are good
for us. Some Christians are like little children—they only
want to eat that which is good TO them, but not
necessarily that which is good FOR them. And Mom
says, "Eat your spinach, honey." And then we hear a
further word, "Eat ALL of it!" It is good for you.

> *"And I went unto the angel, and said unto him,
> 'Give me the little book.' And he said unto me, 'Take
> it, and eat it up; and it shall make thy belly
> BITTER, but it shall be in thy mouth SWEET as
> honey'... and it was in my mouth sweet as honey:
> and as soon as I had eaten it, my belly was bitter"
> (Rev. 10:9-10; Ezek. 3:1-3).*

God told John and Ezekiel to eat the Word. Learn this principle: in your mouth the Word is sweet like honey, but in your belly, in your innermost being, it becomes bitter. Some of you have begun to taste of the painful reality of what it means to be crucified with Christ. We will never fellowship the power of His resurrection in our lives until we have fellowshipped the sufferings of our Lord (Gal. 2:20; Phil. 3:8-11). Some of you are running from that. So God has arranged for you to hear this so you can repent and change your mind and get on the right track.

I want you to be an overcomer. I really do. I don't want you to be filled with frustration. I learned something a long time ago: if you want to know what the Bible means, then first see what the Bible SAYS. "We went through all that GREAT and TERRIBLE wilderness." Now, instead of that word "wilderness," insert that person or thing that God has custom-built for YOUR development. I know what is happening to you who are crying out in your spirit to be like the Lord: you are being processed and matured and trained and changed!

One extreme in the land proclaims the great things. The other tangent can only project the terrible things. I believe in faith and prosperity, but I also believe in the wilderness dealings that will make these truths work themselves out in reality and practicality.

THE KEY TO LIFE: A RIGHT SPIRIT

"For the Lord thy God hath BLESSED thee in all the works of thy hand: He KNOWETH thy walking THROUGH this great wilderness: these forty years the Lord thy God hath been with thee; THOU HAST LACKED NOTHING" (Deut. 2:7).

Praise His Name! Isn't that wonderful? We should

rejoice! God can furnish a table in the wilderness (Psa.
78:19). In the presence of your enemies your cup will run
over (Psa. 23:5). God is faithful in the wilderness. He
knows every step that we have taken. He knows the way
that we take.

The wilderness is the way to life. The majority die in
the wilderness. We must mix the Word with faith (Heb.
4:2). We must walk in what we have heard. God has done
all that He can do. All that remains is the KEY to life,
the key to Canaan:

WE MUST MAINTAIN A RIGHT SPIRIT
AND A RIGHT ATTITUDE AT ALL TIMES!

What is your RESPONSE to the dealings of God? Are
you angry and bitter, filled with resentment and rage?
Or are you thankful and broken? What is in your spirit?
What is your attitude?

The carnal mind says, "I see no value or purpose to the
wilderness." The carnal mind is looking for a loophole.
The carnal mind doesn't like it or want it. The Mind of
Christ, the spiritual mind of Rom. 8:1-6, knows that the
servant is not above his Lord. The disciple is not above
his Master (Matt. 10:24; Lk. 6:40).

God is looking for a people who cannot be moved or
upset by anything. The cry of His heart is for a people
who can share His throne and shepherd the nations with
a rod of iron (Rev. 2:26-28). We cannot afford the luxury
of our personal feelings. We have no rights. If we do,
we'll lose them in the wildreness! Your testings will last
as long as it takes to change your mind and attitude. Can
we walk around in the furnace without complaining? Can
we sing in the fire? The key to God's whole program
operating in your life is your spirit and attitude of
response to His Word for your life.

*"Wherefore glorify ye the Lord in the fires" (Isa.
24:15).*

The principle is this: out of Egypt, THROUGH the wilderness, and into the land. We will never enjoy our full inheritance until we have experienced the wilderness. Do you want to be an overcomer? Then look at the Pattern.

JESUS WENT THROUGH THE WILDERNESS

If our ministries are to be effective, we must center everything that we do and teach in JESUS (Col. 3:17). Our message must be Christ-centered. Do you want to be like Jesus? Do you believe that He is the Pattern Son? Then understand that Jesus went THROUGH the wilderness!

First of all, Jesus was BORN OF THE SPIRIT. Did you realize that? He was conceived and begotten of the Holy Ghost:

"The HOLY GHOST shall come upon thee, and the power of the Highest shall overshadow thee: therefore also that holy thing which shall be born of thee shall be called the SON OF GOD" (Lk. 1:35).

Secondly, Jesus was BAPTIZED IN WATER. This, too, is not an option, for He is the Prototype of all sons:

"Now when all the people were baptized, it came to pass, that Jesus also being BAPTIZED ..." (Lk. 3:21).

Thirdly, Jesus was FILLED WITH THE HOLY GHOST (Acts 10:38). What He received at the Jordan was more than what we received in the Pentecostal experience, which is but the firstfruits of the Spirit and the earnest of our inheritance (Rom. 8:23; Eph. 1:13-14). He received the Spirit without measure, the fullness of the Godhead bodily (Jn. 3:34; Col. 2:9). But the principle is there: Jesus was born of the Spirit, and baptized in water, and filled with the Holy Ghost (Lk. 3:21-22).

Jesus was conceived by the Spirit; so were you. He was baptized in water; so were many of you. He was filled with the Holy Ghost; so were many of you. This fulfills the foundation of Acts 2:38 in the life of the believer:

"Repent, and be baptized every one of you in the name of Jesus Christ for the remission of sins, and ye shall receive the gift of the Holy Ghost."

Then what happened to the Pattern? The same thing that must happen to every one of us who have been converted and baptized in water and in the Holy Ghost:

"And Jesus being full of the Holy Ghost, returned from Jordan, and was LED by the Spirit into the WILDERNESS... And immediately the Spirit DRIVETH him into the wilderness" (Lk. 4:1; Mk. 1:12).

Jesus was led by the Spirit into the wilderness! Isn't it rather odd that some of those who profess to be sent with HIS Word would tell you otherwise? Note that the Gospel of Mark states that Jesus was DRIVEN into the place of testing. Let's allow the Lord to do the driving. Let Him be your chauffeur.

Jesus is the Pattern. He was tempted and tested and overcame in three areas or dimensions. The Bible lists these three principles as follows:

"Love not the world, neither the things that are in the world. If any man love the world, the love of the Father is not in him. For ALL that is in the world, THE LUST OF THE FLESH, and THE LUST OF THE EYES, and THE PRIDE OF LIFE, is not of the Father, but is of the world. And the world passeth away, and the lust thereof: but he that

doeth the will of God abideth for ever" (1 Jn. 2:15-17).

Like Jesus, we must also be proven in these three principles. I'm glad that you are saved. I'm thrilled that you are filled with the Holy Ghost. Now learn the purpose of Pentecost. What is on the other side of that wilderness?

"And Jesus returned in the POWER of the Spirit into Galilee: and there went out a fame of him through all the region round about" (Lk. 4:14).

"Then Jesus, armed with the power of the Spirit, returned to Galilee" (New English Bible).

Compare the verses given above with Acts 1:8 and you will discover a tremendous principle:

"But ye shall receive POWER, AFTER THAT the Holy Ghost is come upon you: and ye shall be witnesses unto me both in Jerusalem, and in all Judea, and in Samaria, and unto the uttermost part of the earth."

You shall receive POWER "after that." After what? Follow the Pattern in Luke 4 and you will know the answer. He "returned" from the place of being proven in the POWER of the Spirit. The Greek word for "power" is "DUNAMIS" (compare the words dynamite, dynamo, dynamic). It is #1411 and is found 120 times in the New Testament—compare the 120 in the upper room (Acts 1:15). It is rendered as "ability, abundance, mighty deeds, might, mightily, mighty, miracle, workers of miracles, power, strength, violence, virtue, mighty works, wonderful works."

Why don't we see these things in the churches? Because nobody wants the wilderness experience that

will produce it. Two things are lacking in the Church
world today that are evident if you read the Book of
Acts. Number one, the POWER. Number two, the
PRICE to get it. These signs shall follow them that
believe (Mk. 16:15-20). If we don't see these things, then
we simply do not believe.

The Pattern was tested in the area of the LUST OF
THE FLESH (Lk. 4:1-4). This deals with the realm of
self-satisfaction. Some use the anointing for their selfish
gain. What WE want. The devil said, "If thou be the son
of God, command this stone that it be made bread." But
Jesus wouldn't do it. He quoted Deut. 8:3 and overcame
in this realm. And we must do the same (Rev. 3:21).

Jesus was tested in the area of the LUST OF THE
EYES (Lk. 4:5-8). This speaks of materialism and the
love of money (1 Tim. 6:10). Some use the anointing to
make money and merchandise of God's people (2 Pet.
2:3). Jesus refused the glitter of the world systems,
quoted Deut. 6:13; 10:20, and won the second round. A
true son cannot be bought.

Thirdly, the Lord was tested in the area of the PRIDE
OF LIFE (Lk. 4:9-13). We must be dealt with in these
three dimensions. Some use the anointing to be seen of
men and to receive man-worship. They want to be
popular. Jesus quoted Psa. 91:11 and Deut. 6:16,
overcoming the Evil One by the Word of God.

Jesus made himself of no reputation (Phil 2:1-11). He
was not interested in being seen of men; therefore, He
could not be hid (Matt. 5:14; Mk. 7:24). I want to be like
Jesus, don't you? The Church is the light of the world. It
is to be made up of people who are radiating HIM so that
men can't see anything or anyone else but Jesus.

> *"And there were certain Greeks among them that
> came up to worship at the feast: the same came
> therefore to Philip, which was of Bethsaida of
> Galilee, and desired him, saying, 'Sir, we would see
> JESUS" (Jn. 12:20-21).*

THE JUBILEE MINISTRY ON THE
OTHER SIDE OF THE WILDERNESS

Follow the Pattern. He was proven in the three realms given above and was an Overcomer by the Word. "It is written!" On the other side of that wilderness was a Jubilee ministry of great deliverance. Jubilee (#3104) means "the blast of a horn (from its continuous sound); the signal of the silver trumpets; hence the instrument itself and the festival thus introduced; jubile, ram's horn, trumpet." The ROOT word (#2986) means "to flow; to bring (with pomp); bring forth, carry, lead forth."

The Theological Wordbook of the Old Testament says, "This word ("yobel") is distinct from "shopar" which is the general and most common word for any kind of trumpet or horn. Some think the "yobel" in Joshua 6 refers to the same "horn" that is employed at the beginning of the year of Jubilee. On the other hand, this noun in Leviticus (25:9-15,28-33,40,50-54; 27:17-24) and Numbers (36:4) is never translated, but transliterated by the word "jubilee." The context of these passages is the YEAR OF JUBILEE when the land lies fallow, all possessions (especially the land, its produce, and slaves) revert to the ORIGINAL OWNERS, and produce is provided for the people by Yahweh's blessing upon the land in the previous year; therefore, it seems that the derivation of "jubilee" is probably from "yabal" (to bring forth). The produce is brought forth to provide for the fallow jubilee year, and property is brought or RETURNED to the original owners. The "year of Jubilee" begins with the blast of the "shopar" of the Day of Atonement each fiftieth year. It is a year that is holy (separated) unto Yahweh."

The possession is returned to the original owner. In the light of present truth, man is going to inherit the earth (Gen. 1:26-28; Matt. 5:5; Psa. 2:8; Rev. 2:26-28). The Jubilee ministry is a ministry that DELIVERS THE CREATION (Rom. 8:14-23). Jesus Christ is the

Pattern of such a ministry. After the necessity of being tested, the Lord went into His home town, and His "home church," and said,

> *"The Spirit of the Lord is upon me, because he hath ANOINTED me to preach the gospel to the POOR: he hath sent me to heal the BROKENHEARTED, to preach deliverance to the CAPTIVES, and recovering of sight to the BLIND, to set at liberty them that are BRUISED, to preach the ACCEPTABLE YEAR of the Lord" (Lk. 4:18)*

The "acceptable Year of the Lord" is "year of LIBERTY" (Ezek. 46:17; compare Is. 61:1; Lev. 25:10) which is the Year of Jubilee. This ministry of Jesus operated on the other side of the wilderness experience. Only a free man can set a man free. We are called to be proven and then to deliver the creation.

All slaves were released in the Year of Jubilee. Prison doors swung open. The Lord Jesus came to inaugurate this ministry of deliverance. He came to liberate in five dimensions. He came to deliver the:

1. BEGGAR ("the poor")
2. BROKENHEARTED
3. BOUND ("the captives")
4. BLIND
5. BRUISED

You and I are called to deliver the BEGGARS. Throw away your tin cup and then throw away your beggar's garment. A lot of folks want God to "touch" them. Why don't you get FILLED with Him? Hallelujah! Jesus is King of KINGS and Lord of LORDS (Rev. 19:16). We are to be kings and priests, not beggars.

You and I are called to deliver the BROKENHEART-ED. The joy of the Lord is your strength (Neh. 8:10). Let us go forth and exchange somebody's spirit of heaviness for a garment of praise (Isa. 61:3). Let us be filled with the oil of gladness, and then dispense His life and strength to others.

You and I are called to deliver the BOUND. This is a spiritual warfare. There are many different spirits that are binding people. We are called to cast out devils (Mk. 16:17). Many sit in a prisonhouse of their own making. Their own conceit, and self-pity, and rebellion, and resentment, and bitterness has shackled their mind and spirit. Let us set them free in the Name of the Lord!

You and I are called to deliver the BLIND. This is true in the natural and in the spirit. Our eyes have been opened to the dealings and the purposes of God. Let us lift the scales of unbelief from the understanding of others (Eph. 1:18). We who have become blind that we might see are sent to help others (Acts 9:8-19).

You and I are called to deliver the BRUISED. I am not speaking of those who are squealing under the rod of discipline or correction, but those who have been tossed and buffeted by the enemy. Like the Pattern, we must be gentle in ministering life to these who have been wounded (Matt. 12:20).

God wants to give you your city. God wants to give you your local area. God wants to fill us with the Holy Ghost and flow through us in deliverance. But we must know what it is to press through the wilderness. We must know what it is to be overcomers.

On the other side of the wilderness is a great ministry. For those who learn to overcome the wilderness and maintain a right spirit, there is a partaking and sharing of the ministry of Jesus.

On the other side of the wilderness is great satisfaction. We have been led by the Spirit into the dealings of God. Everything that God has worked into us has been deposited for the benefit of someone else. We have been delivered from our selfishness in the wilderness.

On the other side of the wilderness there is a great

peace. It wasn't meant to be easy. The Kingdom of God
is not for half-hearted people. We love not our lives unto
the death (Rev. 12:11). Our tribulation is over, and now
we can minister to those who are in tribulation (2 Cor.
1:3-5).

On the other side of the wilderness there is a great joy.
We have endured the cross, despising the shame (Heb.
12:2). The joy and the privilege of sharing the nature and
the ministry of Jesus becomes a reality on the other side
of the wilderness.

HOW TO SHORTEN YOUR
WILDERNESS EXPERIENCE

How long was Israel in the wilderness? Forty years
(Ex. 16:35; Num. 14:33-34; 32:13; Deut. 2:7; 8:2,4; 29:5;
Josh. 5:6; Neh. 9:21; Psa. 95:10; Acts 7:36,42; Heb.
3:9,17). How long was JESUS in the wilderness? Forty
days (Matt. 4:2; Mark 1:13; Luke 4:2). Which do you
want? Forty years or forty days? Would you like to
shorten your wilderness experience?

I guarantee you that you will have a wilderness
experience if you follow on to know the Lord. How will
you respond? How long will it take you to get through
the wilderness?

How did Jesus get through the wilderness? By saying,
"IT IS WRITTEN!" He knew the Word. He WAS the
Word (Jn. 1:1,14)! He is the Pattern. He is the Living
Word. He overcame the Evil One by the Word.

We must know the Word. We, too, must BECOME the
Word. Once again the Word of God is becoming flesh,
and dwelling among men. The principle is seen in the
NAME of Emmanuel (Isa. 7:14; Matt. 1:23) which means
"God with us." The Word was God. God was the Word.
You are kings (Rev. 1:6). You are lords (Rev. 19:16; Gal.
4:1; Dan. 2:47). You are gods (Psa. 82:6; Jn. 10:34).

"Herein is our love made perfect, that we may have boldness in the day of judgment: because AS HE IS, so are WE in this world" (1 Jn. 4:17).

"... for we realize that our life in this world is actually His life lived in us" (Phillips).

"... since in this world we are living as He lives" (Moffatt).

"... because even in this world we have become as He is" (Jerusalem Bible).

Two other passages of Scripture show us how to shorten our experience in the wilderness:

"For the [true] love of God is this, that we do His commands—keep His ordinances and are mindful of His precepts and teaching. And these orders of His are not irksome—burdensome, oppressive or grievous. For whatever is born of God is victorious over the world; and this is the victory that CONQUERS the world, even our FAITH" (1 Jn. 5:3-4—The Amplified Bible).

"Those who prove victorious I will allow to share My throne, JUST AS I was victorious Myself and took My place with My Father on His throne. If anyone has ears to listen, let him listen to what the Spirit is saying to the churches" (Rev. 3:21-22—The Jerusalem Bible).

We are to conquer the world as Jesus did. The world is the lust of the flesh, the lust of the eyes, and the pride of life. Jesus overcame by knowing and being the WORD!

You and I can shorten our stay in the dealings of God. We will stay in that heavenly woodshed until we know the Word and become what we know. So don't get your

eyes on the tempter or what he offers. Get your eyes and
your mind on the Word! JESUS is the Word! Some
never learn this Word. Some learn this Word but never
become what they know. There is a multitude of
groaning people on the other side of the wilderness.
Hasten to help them!

Let me remind you again of Deut. 8:2. God is doing a
work in our lives and He is doing it in the wilderness.

> *"And you shall (earnestly) remember all the way
> which the Lord your God led you these forty years
> in the wilderness, to humble you, and to prove you,
> to know what was in your [mind and] heart, whether
> you would keep His commandments or not"*
> *(Amplified Bible).*

God knows from the beginning that we can make it.
But He wants US to know! We have been led through
tribulation that we might see ourselves from the lofty
viewpoint of the Mind of the Spirit. We must learn to see
ourselves and others as God does. In order to do this we
must be broken and our natural understanding brought
to nought (1 Cor. 1:18-30; 2:9-14).

How can we know the greatness of this Christ in us if
we are never tested? We must experience in reality the
truth that greater is He Who is in us than he who is
trying to get us (1 Jn. 4:4)! This is the Day of the Lord,
and EVERYONE is being tried by fire.

Let me give you an example from the natural realm.
Have you noticed the ever-increasing number of
products that are being RECALLED to the factory
because of some defect or malfunction? An
embarrassing mistake could have been prevented if that
product had been THOROUGHLY TESTED before
being placed on the market for public use. A lot of time
and money is wasted, and all of us are shortchanged. We
are seeing the same thing happen in the spiritual realm.
There are many "ministries" who are out on the market

for public consumption. Many have not been tested. All the ministries of the Book of Acts were PROVEN ministries. They were discipled by the older ministries in the context of the local church. For those today who have not seen the need of being pressed through tribulations I will not be surprised if God recalls you back to His factory for further inspection and adjusting.

WATER OUT OF THE ROCK OF FLINT

"Who led thee THROUGH that great and terrible wilderness, wherein were fiery serpents, and scorpions, and DROUGHT, where there was NO WATER; who brought thee forth water out of the rock of flint" (Deut. 8:15).

We fear the wilderness because we fear the DROUGHT. We fear the place of NO WATER. The place of testing necessitates a miraculous provision. The word rendered as "DROUGHT" (#6774) means "a thirsty place; desert, drought, dry ground, or thirsty land" (Isa. 35:7).

Thirst was especially felt during the siege of a city. With the major supplies of water cut off, the besieged had to ration their water (Lam. 4:4). It is in the wilderness that the Lordship of Jesus lays siege to the strongholds of our carnality and the vain imaginations of our natural minds (2 Cor. 10:3-5). Most people remain in the security of Egypt, but there are those who have been loosed from that bondage by the blood of the Passover Lamb!

I have shown that the natural nation was a pattern for the New Testament nation. God is bringing a BODY of people forth in this hour who have experienced what Paul revealed to the Corinthians. We will have to bring forth water out of the rock of flint.

> *"Moreover, brethren, I would not that ye should be
> ignorant, how that all our fathers were under the
> cloud, and all passed through the sea; and were all
> baptized unto Moses in the cloud and in the sea; and
> did all eat the same spiritual meat; and did all
> DRINK the same SPIRITUAL DRINK: for they
> drank of that spiritual ROCK that followed them:
> and that Rock was CHRIST ... Now all these
> things happened unto them for ensamples: and they
> are written for our admonition, upon whom the ends
> of the world are come" (1 Cor. 10:1-4,11).*

The key word to this passage is "ALL." There are no
options if we are to be a part of the holy nation that He is
leading (1 Pet. 2:9-10). There are FIVE EXPERIENCES
that are mentioned here.

Three of these experiences are ONCE-FOR-ALL in
nature:

1. BLOOD.
2. BAPTISM IN WATER.
3. BAPTISM IN THE HOLY GHOST.

Two of these experiences are CONTINUOUS in
nature:

4. BREAD.
5. BEVERAGE.

We have been delivered by the BLOOD, the WATER,
and the SPIRIT (1 Jn. 5:8). As noted above, we have
been saved by the blood of Jesus the Lamb (Ex. 12:1-14;
1 Cor. 5:7). Then we must understand that this first
experience is not enough. Just as Israel was baptized
into Moses at the Red Sea (Ex. 14-15) and in the cloud
(Ex. 13), so we have been baptized into Christ in water
and in the Holy Ghost. Moses was the mediator of the
Old Covenant (Gal. 3:19). JESUS is the Mediator of the

New Testament (1 Tim. 2:5). Moses was the head of the Old Testament nation. JESUS is the Head of the New Testament nation, the Church (Eph. 1:22; Col. 1:18). Moses became a many-membered man: God multiplied Moses into a nation. JESUS is becoming a Corporate, Many-membered, New Creation Man (Eph. 4:13)! We were not baptized into Moses. We were baptized into Christ. There are three experiences that God wants EVERY Christian to enjoy: the blood, the water, and the Spirit. Have you been washed in the blood? Have you sealed that conversion with water baptism in the Name of the Lord? Have you received the Holy Ghost since you believed (Acts 19:2)?

The foundation of Acts 2:38 is not enough (Heb. 6:1-3). Have you discovered the purpose of Pentecost? You'll learn that secret in the wilderness! For over 80 years, men have cried "Lord, I hope your blessings FALL tonight!" If you are filled with the Holy Ghost, God's power HAS fallen on you! In fact, it fell and the Comforter was given almost 2000 years ago.

The overcoming saint must walk in two more experiences that are CONTINUAL: the BREAD and the BEVERAGE. You know that we must daily eat the Bread of Life, the Word of God (Jn. 6). As Israel gathered manna in the wilderness (Ex. 16), so pray for our daily Bread (Matt. 6:11). You need to devour that Bible. You need to set aside times when you and your family can read AND study God's Word. You need to be part of a local church where the LIVING Word is proclaimed by those who have been sent from the Lord. This is something that we must do habitually. It is a way of life.

"Man shall not live by bread alone, but by every word that proceedeth out of the mouth of God" (Matt. 4:4).

The BEVERAGE is the sweet, living water of the

Holy Ghost from WITHIN the life of the believer. Those
who have never learned this still want the Holy Ghost to
come DOWN, but there is a WELL in you that needs to
spring UP!

> *"And from thence they went to Beer: that is the*
> *WELL whereof the Lord spake unto Moses, 'Gather*
> *the people together, and I will give them water.'*
> *Then Israel SANG this song, 'SPRING UP, O*
> *WELL; Sing ye unto it: the princes digged the well,*
> *the nobles of the people digged it, by the direction of*
> *the lawgiver, with their staves' " (Num. 21:16-17).*

We sing the chorus:

> "Spring up, O well, within my soul!
> Spring up, O well, and make me whole!
> Spring up, O well, and give to me
> That life abundantly!"

> "I've got a river of life flowing out of me,
> It makes the lame to walk and the blind to see,
> It opens prison doors and sets the captive free,
> I've got a river of life flowing out of me!"

One of the grandest truths revealed in the wilderness
is this WELL! We learn to DRINK in the wilderness.
The well from within is the secret to pressing through
our tribulations. Let us bring forth water from the rock
of flint, and that rock is the CHRIST! Christ IN you, the
hope of glory (Col. 1:27)!

Only GOD can make a flinty rock. This well from
within us was placed there by God and not by man. The
reason why God brings Spirit-filled Christians through
trials and testings is that they can learn how to drink
continually from the Spirit within. Instead of panicking
and calling the preacher every time, draw water from the
well within! Many cry, "Oh, if I can just get to the man

of God!" Well, that is good, and thank God for men of God who will pray for you, but there is something better than the gifts of God flowing through the hands of a man. The Healer is WITHIN you! The Life is IN you! The Christ is WITHIN you!

> *"Therefore with JOY shall ye draw water out of the wells of salvation... Sing unto the Lord... For great is the Holy One of Israel in the MIDST of thee" (Isa. 12:3-4,6).*

> *"Joyfully then shall you draw upon the FOUNTAINS of deliverance" (Moffatt).*

> *"Oh, the joy of drinking deeply from the fountain of salvation" (Taylor).*

> *"... from the SPRINGS of salvation" (The Jerusalem Bible).*

Learn to pray in the power of the Holy Ghost. Learn to drink and to build yourself up (1 Cor. 14:4,14-18; Rom. 8:26-27; Eph. 6:18; Jude 20). Unless we learn to walk through the wilderness, we will never learn to drink the BEVERAGE of the Spirit from within, and we will miss the purpose of Pentecost. Don't get your eyes on the desolate wilderness. You are walking with the Fountain of Life. There is a leaping fountain that will spring up into everlasting life (Jn. 4:14). God has provided a table in the wilderness. Drink, and drink abundantly, beloved (Psa. 78:19; Song of Solomon 5:1).

We learn to PRAY in the wilderness. We learn how to PRAISE and WORSHIP in the wilderness. Our devotional life before the Lord is the KEY to our pressing on through tribulation. There is a SUPERNATURAL SUPPLY in the place of trial. There is a fountain of life in the midst of death and desolation.

Let the Christ from within you leap up and over every circumstance. You are filled with His omnipotence, but how will you ever know it until you prove it (Rom. 12:1-2)? Release the God from within you by SINGING to the well, for He is:

"... *able to do exceeding abundantly above all that we ask or think, according to the POWER THAT WORKETH IN US" (Eph. 3:20).*

YOUR HELP IS WITHIN YOU

Most of the Church world is seeking deliverance from an EXTERNAL source. Most are seeking help from the wrong direction. This is manifested in two ways:

1. Some are looking for the Lord Jesus to come at any minute to catch them away and thus solve all their problems. The Lord Jesus is coming, and the Second Coming is very real, but let us examine our motives. Are we looking for a "fire escape?"

2. Some are looking for some fiery prophet to come down the road and lay his hands on them and prophesy away their problems in a moment of time. Fiery prophets and the laying on of hands and prophecy are very real, but we need once more to check our motives and attitudes.

Your help and deliverance and salvation will NOT come from without. The Father raised Jesus from the dead, but the Father was WITHIN Jesus! Your deliverance will come from WITHIN. Your help is within you.

"Is not my help IN me?" (Job 6:13).

"Is not my help WITH me?" (Young's Literal Translation).

The key to this is the SPOKEN WORD. Your words, filled with faith and in agreement with His Word, will release the Kingdom of God from within you. Consider this:

> *"For this COMMANDMENT... is not hidden from thee, neither is it FAR OFF. It is NOT in heaven, that thou shouldest say, 'Who shall go up for us to heaven, and bring it unto us, that we may hear it, and do it?' NEITHER is it beyond the sea, that thou shouldest say, 'Who shall go over the sea for us, and bring it unto us, that we may hear it, and do it?' But the WORD is NIGH thee, in thy MOUTH, and in thy HEART, that thou mayest do it... But the righteousness which is of faith SPEAKETH... The WORD is nigh thee, even in thy MOUTH, and in thy HEART: that is, the WORD of faith which we preach"* (Deut. 30:11-14; Rom. 10:6-10).

> *"For salvation... is already within easy reach of each of us; in fact, it is as near as our own hearts and mouths"* (Rom. 10:8—Taylor).

> *"Near you the word is, in your mouth and in your heart"* (Wuest).

This is why the Lord has emphasized the importance of our WORDS in the last fifteen years. And where is it that we learn to rise up and speak the living Word? In the wilderness! We must learn to speak and decree our own deliverance. The anointing is in you. Rise and declare the Word of the Lord! There are many passages of Scripture that are birthed in our spirit in the place of testing. By the power and authority of these faith-filled words, we can press through tribulation.

> *"Thou shalt also DECREE a thing, and it shall be established unto thee"* (Job 22:28).

*"Thou art snared with THE WORDS OF THY
MOUTH, thou art taken with THE WORDS OF
THY MOUTH" (Prov. 6:2).*

*"... for out of the abundance of the heart the mouth
SPEAKETH" (Mt. 12:34).*

*"A wholesome TONGUE is a tree of life" (Prov.
15:4).*

*"For by THY WORDS thou shalt be justified, and
by THY WORDS thou shalt be condemned" (Mt.
12:37).*

This should be obvious, but we will say that this entire
message emphasizes the RESPONSIBILITY of every
Christian to grow up and take hold of God for himself.
That is one reason why the Gospel of The Kingdom
won't win a popularity contest. Take it from one who has
discovered these truths firsthand, it is a marvelous thing
when YOU can pray, and God will hear and answer. I
promise you this: He is not going to take you out of your
problems. He is going to rise up from within you and
declare a living Word! God is going to bring you through
your circumstances and prove His power and might to
be real in YOUR life!

ANOTHER COMFORTER

You are not walking through the wilderness alone.
Isn't that wonderful? There is One who has been sent to
come with you and bear you up on eagle wings!
I am amazed at the number of believers who want to
go through life without experiencing the ministry of the
Comforter. Perhaps that is the reason why so many are
still self-centered and selfish. They couldn't care less
about the needs of the other fellow. They have not

reached out in mercy and comfort to others because they are empty and void of His comfort. They have never known what it means to be comforted by the Holy Ghost. Every time a hard place comes the carnal mind drags them further into spiritual, emotional, and mental bondage. They look for a way out. These folk will run to the next town, the next church, the next job, the next ministry, the next doctor . . . whatever is convenient. They refuse to mature. Anything negative that crosses their will is avoided with scheme after scheme energized by the fleshy mind that is hostile toward God (Rom. 8:1-6).

Some of you are running. Do you know what you will find when you stop? The thing that you have seemingly escaped is STILL THERE. You carried it with you. It is WITHIN you. The moment you stop running, the Comforter is going to catch up to you and help you become an overcomer. Turn to God in sincerity, and let Him help you and deal with you.

> *"And I will pray the Father, and He shall give you another COMFORTER, that He may abide with you for ever; even the Spirit of truth; whom the world cannot receive, because it seeth Him not, neither knoweth Him; for He dwelleth with you, and shall be IN you. . . But the COMFORTER, which is the HOLY GHOST, whom the Father will send in My name, He shall teach you all things, and bring all things to your remembrance, whatsoever I have said unto you" (Jn. 14:16-17,26).*

The Comforter is the Holy Ghost. You will get to know Him in the dry places of the wilderness. You will learn to hear His still, small voice in the silence of the desert. In the loneliness of the dealings of God, we learn to hear the voice of the Spirit. He is the Comforter.

The Greek word for "Comforter" is "PARAKLETOS" (#3875) and is found five times in the New Testament

(Jn. 14:16,26; 15:26; 16:7; 1 Jn. 2:1). The last reference is rendered as "ADVOCATE." The principle of the comforter is unique to John's writing. Note the various meanings of this word:

1. Strong—"an intercessor, consoler; advocate, comforter."

2. Vine—"called to one's side, to one's aid, is primarily a verbal adjective, and suggests the capability or adaptability of giving aid. It was used in a court of justice to denote a legal assistant, counsel for the defense, an advocate ... it signifies a succourer, comforter."

3. Thayer—"summoned, called to one's side, especially, called to one's aid; one who pleads another's cause before a judge, a pleader, counsel for defense, legal assistant, an advocate; one who pleads another's cause with one, an intercessor; a helper, succorer, aider, assistant."

4. Vincent—"from PARA, to the side of, and KALEO, to summon; it means more than a mere CONSOLER, being derived from the Latin CONFORTARE, to strengthen ... our Advocate, or Counsel, 'who suggests true reasoning to our minds, and true courses of action for our lives, who convicts our adversary, the world, or wrong, and pleads our cause before God our Father.' It is to be noted that JESUS as well as the HOLY SPIRIT is represented as Paraclete."

5. Bullinger—"called to one's aid ... he who has been or may be called to help."

6. Alford—"Thus the idea of help and strength is conveyed by it, as well as of consolation."

7. Bengel—"The verb PARAKALEIN is the Latin ADVOCARE, to summon a patron; thence comes PARAKLATOS, one summoned to aid; one's defender, patron; who speaks for him, and suggests to him what to say."

8. Wuest—". . . the Counsellor, the Holy Spirit" (Jn. 14:26).

We must press through tribulation. The ministry of the Holy Ghost enables us to be an overcomer in the place of trial. Consider the words of the apostle:

"Blessed be the God and Father of our Lord Jesus Christ, the Father of tender mercies and the God of all comfort, who comforts me in all my distress, so that I am able to comfort people who are in any distress by the comfort with which I myself am comforted by God. For as the sufferings of Christ are abundant in my case, so my comfort is also abundant through Christ. If I am in distress, it is in the interests of your comfort and salvation; if I am comforted, it is in the interests of your comfort, which is effective as it nerves you to endure the same sufferings as I endure myself" (2 Cor. 1:3-6—Moffatt).

Do you see now why the wilderness is necessary? It is to open you up so that you can minister to the needs of others. Get to know the Comforter, and then introduce Him to others as they see and feel His effectual working in you.

"THROUGH"

Let me highlight the key principles of several passages that contain the word "THROUGH." God is not going to take us out, but He is going to bring us through!

"And thou didst divide the sea before them, so that they went THROUGH the midst of the sea on the dry land; and their persecutors thou threwest into the deeps, as a stone into the mighty waters" (Neh. 9:11).

God is not only doing something for you as He brings you through tribulation. He is also destroying your persecutors and pursuers. Your enemies are His enemies. God is very efficient. He develops you and destroys His enemies at the same time.

"For thou wilt light my candle: the Lord my God will enlighten my darkness. For by thee I have run THROUGH a troop; and by my God have I leaped over a wall" (Psa. 18:28-29).

You are called to be an overcomer. Come over that wall. Mount that obstacle! You are the light of the world (Mt. 5:14). You can run or break through every problem because of the strength and the joy of the Lord (Neh. 8:10).

"He turned the sea into dry land: they went THROUGH the flood on foot... For thou, O God, has proved us: thou has tried us, as silver is tried. Thou broughtest us into the net; thou laidst affliction upon our loins. Thou hast caused men to ride over our heads; we went THROUGH fire and THROUGH water: but Thou broughtest us out into a wealthy place" (Psa. 66:6,10-12).

God brings us through the Red Sea and the Jordan at flood tide. On the other side of a great struggle is a great harvest. This wealthy place is a place of "freedom" according to several sources. This is the portion of the overcomer.

> *"Blessed is the man whose strength is in Thee; in whose heart are the ways of them. Who passing THROUGH the valley of Baca maketh it a well; the rain also filleth the pools. They go from strength to strength, every one of them in Zion appeareth before God" (Psa. 84:5-7).*

Baca means "weeping." You will make your valley of weeping a place of springs. The valley of Baca becomes the valley of Berachah, which means "blessing" (2 Chron. 20:26). The overcomer will appear in Zion (Rev. 14:1-5).

> *"Our fathers understood not thy wonders in Egypt; they remembered not the multitude of Thy mercies; but provoked Him at the sea, even at the Red Sea. Nevertheless He saved them for His name's sake, that He might make His mighty power to be known. He rebuked the Red Sea also, and it was dried up: so He led them THROUGH the depths, as THROUGH the wilderness. And He saved them from the hand of him that hated them, and redeemed them from the hand of the enemy. And the waters covered their enemies: there was not one of them left. Then believed they His words; they sang His praise" (Psa. 106:7-12).*

God is saving us from ourselves. It is for the sake of His name that we are being delivered. He rebuked the Red Sea instead of His people. Every enemy will perish in this dealing. Let us sing His praise!

> *"To him that smote Egypt in their firstborn: for His mercy endureth for ever: with a strong hand, and with a stretched out arm . . . To Him which divided the Red Sea into parts . . . and made Israel to pass THROUGH the midst of it . . . but overthrew Pharaoh and his host in the Red Sea . . . To Him*

which led His people THROUGH the
wilderness...to Him which smote great
kings...and slew famous kings..." (Psa.
136:10-18).

Like the Psalmist, let us get hung up on the note of
mercy. God's mercy flows throughout the wilderness. It
flows through God's hand (Eph. 4:11). In His mercy, God
is smiting every famous king that is within us (2 Cor.
10:3-5).

"Go ye forth of Babylon, flee ye from the Chaldeans,
with a voice of singing declare ye, tell this, utter it
even to the end of the earth; say ye, The Lord hath
redeemed His servant Jacob. And they thirsted not
when He led them THROUGH the deserts: He
caused the waters to flow out of the rock for them:
He clave the rock also, and the waters gushed out.
There is no peace, saith the Lord, unto the wicked"
(Isa. 48:20-22).

God has liberated us from the confusion of Babylon.
Let us sing and declare His power throughout the earth.
The Rock of Ages has been smitten for us that we might
be set free from all wickedness and lawlessness. Praise
His Name!

"That led them THROUGH the deep, as an horse in
the wilderness, that they should not stumble?" (Isa.
63:13).

The Lord has delivered our soul from death, our eyes
from tears, and our feet from falling (Psa. 116:8). We
have been proven and will not stumble (#782—"totter,
waver, falter, stumble, faint, or fall").

"Neither said they, Where is the Lord that brought
us up out of the land of Egypt, that led us

THROUGH the wilderness, THROUGH a land of deserts and pits, THROUGH a land of drought, and of the shadow of death, THROUGH a land that no man passed through, and where no man dwelt? And I brought you into a plentiful country, to eat the fruit thereof and the goodness thereof..." (Jer. 2:6-7).

He has led through the deep darkness of the shadow of death. He has kept us and preserved us from danger and destruction. No man ("Adam") can dwell in the wilderness. Literally, we have been brought into "the land of a Carmel" (Isa. 35:2).

"Also I brought you up from the land of Egypt, and led you forty years THROUGH the wilderness, to possess the land of the Amorite" (Amos 2:10).

Forty is the number of trial and testing. We are to press through tribulation that we might possess the promise. "Ask of me, and I shall give thee the heathen for thine inheritance..." (Psa. 2:8; see also Acts 1:8; Rev. 11:15).

"And I will bring the third part THROUGH the fire, and will refine them as silver is refined, and will try them as gold is tried: they shall call on My name, and I will hear them: I will say, It is My people: and they shall say, The Lord is my God" (Zech. 13:9).

We know that there are three realms in God. His remnant has been led through the fires of purification (Rom. 8:14). HIS people know what it is to press through tribulation. We are His people and He is our God (2 Cor. 6:14-7:1; Rev. 18:1-8).

JACOB WAS CREATED BUT ISRAEL IS FORMED

There is a FORMATION taking place in the earth.

There is something being built into you and me. It is the
nature of the CHRIST (Gal. 4:19). A new creation MAN
is coming together and will stand upon its feet as an
exceeding great army! The wind of God's Holy Ghost is
breathing upon the member of His Body in resurrection
power through the mouth of His prophets (Ezek. 37:1-14;
Joel 2:1-11).

*"But now thus saith the Lord that CREATED thee,
O Jacob, and He that FORMED thee, O Israel. Fear
not: for I have redeemed thee, I have called thee by
thy name; thou art Mine. WHEN thou passest
THROUGH the waters, I will be with thee; and
THROUGH the rivers, they shall not overflow thee:
when thou walkest THROUGH the fire, thou shalt
not be burned; neither shall the flame kindle upon
thee. For I am the Lord thy God, the Holy One of
Israel, thy Saviour..." (Isa. 43:1-3).*

Jacob was created, but Israel is FORMED. This word
is "YATSAR" (#3335) meaning "to press, be narrow; be
in distress or vexed; squeezed into shape; to mold into a
form, especially as a potter; to determine (form a
resolution); fashion, form, frame, make, potter, purpose"
(Strong's Concordance).

The Theological Wordbook of the Old Testament adds,
"While the word occurs in synonymous parallelism with
BARA ("create") and ASA ("make") in a number of
passages, its primary emphasis is on the shaping or
forming of the object involved... When used of divine
agency, the root refers most frequently to God's creative
ability. It describes the function of the divine
Potter... The word also occurs in the sense of God's
framing or devising something in His mind. It is used of
His preordained purposes (2 Kg. 19:25; Isa. 37:26; 46:11;
Psa. 139:16) as well as His current plans (Jer. 18:11). The
root is used of God's forming the nation of Israel in the
sense of bringing it into existence. It is used in this way

only by Isaiah and always connotes God's activity in this regard (Isa. 43:1,7,21; 44:2,21,24)."

The wilderness is a divine must. It is there that we are shaped and conformed to the image of His Son (Rom. 8:28-29). It is there that the Mind of Christ is built into us. It is there His nature, the Israel nature of the prevailer and overcomer (Gen. 32:24-32), is formed in us. Christ comes forth.

Now look at Isa. 43:1-3 again. What is the first word of verse two? "WHEN" ... not IF, but WHEN. Do you remember what Jesus taught in the Sermon on the Mount?

> *"He is like a man building a house, who dug and went down deep, and laid a foundation upon a rock; and WHEN a flood arose, the torrent broke against that house and could not shake or move it, because it had been securely built—founded on a rock" (Lk. 6:48—The Amplified Bible).*

EVERY house is tested (1 Cor. 3:1-15). The place of trial and testing must come to the life and ministry of every Christian. We must be formed. We must be squeezed into shape. We must be molded in the hand of the Potter. We are to be the plan, and purpose, and power of God in the earth.

> *"My little children, of whom I travail in birth again until Christ be FORMED in you" (Gal. 4:19).*

There is something being built. If you desire for Him to construct His nature in your life, then learn this: God will bring you THROUGH! The pressures are increasing, not diminishing. I beseech you in the Name of the Lord to see these principles that I am showing you. God will be with you in the fire and in the water. He will bring you through the wilderness and into the land of His promise. I want you to become an overcoming

Christian. I want you to have a testimony of value. And
Isaiah said, "waters." Not just water, but waters.
Plural. Being tested more than one time. God is causing
us to walk in the reality of Kingdom principle. There has
been far too much rhetoric and not enough of that
reality. Too much talk and not enough walk. The prophet
Ezekiel saw the walking out of these truths:

> "Thou son of man, shew the house to the house of
> Israel, that they may be ashamed of their iniquities:
> and let them MEASURE the PATTERN. And if
> they be ashamed of all that they have done, shew
> them the FORM of the house, and the FASHION
> thereof... This is the law of the house; Upon the
> top of the mountain the whole limit thereof round
> about shall be MOST HOLY... Rise, and
> MEASURE the temple of God, and the altar, and
> them that worship therein... For we dare not make
> ourselves of the number, or compare ourselves with
> some that commend themselves: but they
> MEASURING themselves by themselves, and
> comparing themselves among themselves, are not
> wise... till we all come in the unity of the faith, and
> of the knowledge of the Son of God, unto a perfect
> man, unto the MEASURE of the stature of the
> fulness of Christ" (Ezek. 43:10-12; Rev. 11:1; 2 Cor.
> 10:12; Eph. 4:13).

We must measure the Pattern before we can be part of
the formation. Ezekiel was to show the House to the
house ... JESUS was a HOUSE for the fullness of God
(Jn. 1:14; Col. 2:9). JESUS is the PATTERN! Let us not
measure ourselves by human standards, for HE is the
measure we are coming to!
There is a difference between the PATTERN of the
house and the FORMATION of the house. The Pattern
is Jesus and He is the Blueprint and the Prototype of
every son. We must see Him, and like Isaiah, be ashamed

of our lawlessness. Too many in this hour have only seen the Blueprint. But they have not SUBMITTED to His Lordship. We have not been ashamed of the unholy Ishmaels (Gen. 16:1-4) that we have birthed. When one builds a building in the natural, he makes a plan. Then he PAYS A COSTLY PRICE and begins to build according to that plan. WE must pay the price ... we must submit to the Pattern, or there will never be the FORMATION of His more excellent ministry in our lives (Heb. 8:1-6).

Jacob was created, but Israel was formed. The new nature of the Anointed One is taking shape in a people who are pressing through tribulation. Be encouraged by the words of the prophet. The rivers shall not overflow you. And when you walk through the fire, you will not be burned. Neither shall the flame kindle upon you. Praise His Name!

THE PURPOSE OF THE FURNACE

"So the last shall be first, and the first last: for many be called, but few CHOSEN ... I have CHOSEN thee in the furnace of affliction" (Matt. 20:16; Isa. 48:10).

The third chapter of the book of Daniel is a classic passage. I am tempted to write a verse-by-verse study, but I will highlight the major Kingdom principles that will help you in your daily walk.

"Nebuchadnezzar the king made an IMAGE of gold, whose height was THREESCORE cubits, and the breadth thereof SIX cubits: he set it up ... at what time ye hear the sound of the cornet ... and all kinds of MUSICK, ye fall down and worship the golden image that Nebuchadnezzar the king hath set up: and whoso falleth not down and worshippeth shall the same hour be cast into the midst of a

BURNING FIERY FURNACE... There are certain Jews whom thou has set over the affairs of the province of Babylon, SHADRACH, ME- SHACH, and ABEDNEGO; these men, O king, have not regarded thee... therefore he spake, and commanded that they should heat the FURNACE one SEVEN TIMES more than it was wont to be heated. And he commanded the most mighty men that were in his army to bind... and to cast them into the burning fiery furnace... Then Nebuchad- nezzer... said unto his counsellers, 'Did not we cast three men BOUND into the midst of the fire?... Lo, I see FOUR men LOOSE, WALKING in the midst of the fire, and they have NO hurt; and the FORM of the fourth is like the SON OF GOD' " (Dan. 3:1-25).

Do you remember the words of Him that FORMED Israel? "When thou walkest through the fire, thou shalt not be burned; neither shall the flame kindle upon thee" (Isa. 43:2). This literally happened to the three Hebrew children.

"And the princes, governors, and captains, and the king's counsellers, being gathered together, saw these men, upon whose BODIES the fire had NO POWER, nor was an HAIR of their head singed, neither were their coats changed, nor the SMELL of fire had passed on them... Then the king PROMOTED Shadrach, Meshach, and Abednego, in the province of Babylon... who through faith... quenched the violence of fire" (Dan. 3:27,30; Heb. 11:33-34).

The golden image was marked by the principle of MAN. It was SIXTY cubits high and its breadth was SIX cubits. Six is the number of MAN. There are those today who refuse to bow to the image of MAN when the music plays! There are those who refuse to give first place to the carnal mind and the spirit of antichrist. It is significant that this man-worship was prompted by MUSIC. Much of so-called "Christian" music is not Scriptural and does not glorify and honor the Lord Jesus. They honor what Nebuchadnezzer built: the god of self and the carnal mind. Thank God that three did not bow. Thank God for men today who will not bow. Their blessed lot is a burning fiery furnace. If you find yourself in the fire, rejoice! It is a proof of our sonship and turning from idolatry (Matt. 5:10-12).

The furnace was heated SEVEN times hotter than usual. Seven is God's number and reveals the truth that God's own nature will be produced in the fire. Then, again, God IS the furnace (Gen. 15:17) and God IS the consuming fire (Heb. 12:29)! Specifically, God is the WORD (Jn. 1:1) and the Word is a FIRE (Jer. 23:29).

The attitude of the three Hebrews would cross some contemporary thinking in regard to deliverance. They were ready to believe God to bring them through the fire. Listen to their confession and compare it with a startling, balancing statement of truth from the writer to the Hebrews:

> *"O Nebuchadnezzar, we are not careful to answer thee in this matter. If it be so, our God whom we serve is able to deliver us from the burning fiery furnace, and he will deliver us out of thine hand, O king. BUT IF NOT, be it known unto thee, O king, that we will not serve thy gods, nor worship the golden image which thou hast set up ... and others were tortured, NOT ACCEPTING DELIVERANCE; that they might obtain a better resurrection" (Dan. 3:16-18; Heb. 11:35).*

There are many benefits to the furnace experience. Let me condense them into 4 thoughts:

1. The mighty men of Babylon perish when they cast you into the furnace.

2. You are loosed in the furnace.

3. You will astonish Babylon by walking in the furnace.

4. You will meet Jesus in the furnace.

Babylon (#894) means "confusion" and comes from a root word (#1101) meaning "to overflow or MIX." It is also rendered as "the gate of God." Babylon speaks of religious confusion and a mixture of truth and tradition. This is destroyed by the furnace experience. The mighty men of Babylon, whether demons, or giants of fear and unbelief, are consumed by the flames. When we refuse to walk with the crowd, our strongest shackles and bondages and confusions and frustrations will be destroyed in the fiery Presence of God.

We go into the furnace bound. We come out of the furnace LOOSED and are given a promotion in the government. There is a glorious liberty in the fire. The three Hebrew children "fell down bound" into the flames. It must have been hard to get up. Perhaps they just laid there and let the ropes burn off. Hallelujah!

The god and prince of this world system will be shocked at our deliverance. The rulers of the religious systems will be astonished when they see a people who cannot be moved. The Lord Jesus confounded and shocked the Pharisees of His day. There is an overcoming army on the horizon just like Him!

There were four men in the furnace. Whether you believe that the fourth man was Daniel, or whether you believe that this was a Christophany (an appearance of Christ in the Old Testament), the principle remains: you will meet Jesus in the furnace! "The FORM of the fourth is LIKE the Son of God." The formation of His likeness becomes a reality in the fire.

And note that they were WALKING in the MIDST of the flames. They were not huddled over the the corner complaining about the room temperature. Most would say, "O God, hurry up and turn this heat down!" They were glorifying the Lord in the fires (Isa. 24:15). There is an enabling of the Holy Ghost from within that will let you SING in the fire! Can we walk comfortably in the furnace, or will we respond with anger and bitterness? I pray that we will learn the purpose of the furnace. We have experienced a baptism in water and in the Holy Ghost preparatory to baptism in FIRE that reveals the nature of every man and brings man into the experience of His LORDSHIP. If we suffer with Him, we shall reign with Him. Only those who experience the furnace will be promoted in the government of God. Let us present our bodies as a living sacrifice (Dan. 3:28; Rom. 12:1-2) as we follow on in His purposes.

BUT HE PASSING THROUGH THE MIDST

The Lord Jesus must be the Pattern for every principle that we teach. How did He handle trouble? Did He avoid it or overcome it? Actually, the question is redundant, for He condescended into the realm of death to that end. But let's look at what happened in His ministry in Nazareth:

> *"And all they in the synagogue, when they heard these things, were filled with wrath, and rose up, and thrust Him out of the city, and led Him into the brow of the hill whereon their city was built, that they might cast Him down headlong. But He PASSING THROUGH the midst of them went His way" (Lk. 4:28-30).*

> *"But he walked straight through them all . . ." (New English Bible).*

The same One who passed through that angry crowd

also passed through the heavens (Heb. 4:14). He is the
Overcoming, Risen Lord! Don't be surprised when men
of the flesh rise up and hate the truth. This religious mob
wanted to throw Him over that forty-foot brow of the
hill. HE is the example for us. He pressed THROUGH.
Another instance of this is given in John's Gospel:

> *"Your father Abraham rejoiced to see My day: and
> he saw it, and was glad. Then said the Jews unto
> Him, 'Thou art not yet fifty years old, and hast thou
> seen Abraham?' And Jesus said unto them, 'Verily,
> verily, I say unto you, before Abraham was, I am.'
> Then took they up stones to cast at Him: but Jesus
> hid Himself, and went out of the temple, GOING
> THROUGH the midst of them, and so passed by"*
> *(Jn. 8:56-59).*

We are not going out, we are going THROUGH! When
Jesus faced danger and death, He overcame it by going
through it. Note that in both examples it was the WORD
that brought the trouble. The truth of this Gospel will
bring us into the place of tribulation. Jesus said:

> *"But he that received the seed into stony places, the
> same is he that heareth the WORD, and anon with
> joy receiveth it; yet hath he not root in himself, but
> dureth for a while: for when TRIBULATION or
> PERSECUTION ariseth BECAUSE OF THE
> WORD, by and by he is offended"* (Matt. 13:20-21).

> *"... but, when the word brings trouble or
> persecution, he is at once repelled"* (Moffatt).

> *"And he does not have rootage in himself, but is by
> nature a temporizer, and the pressure of
> circumstances having come, and persecution
> because of the Word, immediately he sees in it that
> of which he disapproves and which hinders him*

from acknowledging its authority" (Wuest's Expanded Translation).

". . . he does not last; let some trial come, or some persecution on account of the word, and he falls away at once" (Jerusalem Bible).

". . . but he doesn't have much depth in his life, and the seeds don't root very deeply, and after a while when trouble comes, or persecution begins because of his beliefs, his enthusiasm fades, and he drops out" (The Living Bible).

". . . straightway he findeth cause of stumbling" (Rotherham).

Don't drop out. Don't die on the operating table. Jonah found a ship because he was looking for one. The Word of the Lord has brought us out of Egypt. The Word of the Lord is bringing us through the wilderness. The Word of the Lord will bring us into the land.

IT IS NECESSARY

"And when they had preached the gospel to that city, and had taught many, they returned again to Lystra, and to Iconium, and Antioch, confirming the souls of the disciples, and exhorting them to continue in the faith, and that we MUST through MUCH TRIBULATION enter into the Kingdom of God" (Acts 14:21-22).

We MUST through much tribulation enter into the Kingdom of God. The word for "MUST" is "DEI" (#1163) and means, "IT IS NECESSARY." It comes from the root word "DEO" (#1210) which means, "TO BIND." We are bound to this principle. Tribulation is necessary if we are to enter the Kingdom of God.

I am exhorting and encouraging you to continue in the faith. You MUST experience tribulation. It is necessary. This word is also used in the following Scriptures:

> *"And He began to teach them, that the Son of man MUST suffer many things, and be rejected of the elders, and of the chief priests, and scribes, and be killed, and after three days rise again" (Mk. 8:31).*

> *"... "I MUST be about My Father's business" (Lk. 2:49).*

> *"I MUST preach the kingdom of God to other cities also: for therefore am I sent" (Lk. 4:43).*

> *"... men OUGHT always to pray, and not to faint" (Lk. 18:1).*

> *"Marvel not that I said unto thee, Ye MUST be born again" (Jn. 3:7).*

> *"He MUST increase, but I MUST decrease" (Jn. 3:30).*

> *"God is a Spirit: and they that worship Him MUST worship Him in spirit and in truth" (Jn. 4:24).*

No student of the Bible in his right spiritual mind would argue any of the examples given above. In every case, "it is necessary." And we MUST enter the Kingdom through tribulation. And what is the Kingdom of God?

> *"For the kingdom of God is not meat and drink; but righteousness, and peace, and joy in the Holy Ghost" (Rom. 14:17).*

The Kingdom of God is not some dry old doctrine. The

Kingdom of God is a present reality. It is a LIFESTYLE filled with RIGHTEOUSNESS and PEACE and JOY. It is a walk in the HOLY GHOST. Get filled with the King. Get enough of Him so that your family and your neighbors can see Him!

We will pay a price for a walk like this. The prophet Daniel said that there would be two kinds of Christians in the end of this age:

1. Those who would be worn out by the beast systems (Dan. 7:25).

2. Those who would be strong and do because they know their God (Dan. 11:25).

The word for "WEAR OUT" in Dan. 7:25 is #1080 and means "to afflict or wear out (in a mental sense);" Wilson, in his Old Testament Word Studies, adds, "to afflict, to vex; to wear out, to persecute with the purpose of entire annihilation."

Going back to the passage in Acts 14, we can see that this is what the Jews tried to do with Paul in verse 19 when they stoned him and dragged him out of the city. He later went back to Lystra, bearing in his body the marks of the Lord. He preached, and demonstrated that we must press through tribulation. Paul was an overcomer. He was not worn out because he knew his God!

Where do you get to know God and His strength? In the valley of humiliation and degradation and heartache and pain. In the wilderness; the place of humiliation and brokenness. In some of those dark, lonely hours when the evil one shoots his fiery darts.

It's not easy. David gave us all some good advice:

". . . but I will surely buy it of thee at a price: neither will I offer burnt offerings unto the Lord my God of that which doth cost me nothing" (2 Sam. 24:24).

YE HAVE NOT PASSED THIS WAY HERETOFORE

This is a great day! This is the Day which the Lord hath made; we will rejoice and be glad in it (Psa. 118:24). If we will dedicate ourselves to God, He'll do exceeding abundantly above all we can ask or think. You will do more than just muddle through, brothers and sisters. You will stand in the battle in the Day of the Lord (Ezek. 13:5). You will stand in the evil day and have boldness in the day of judgment (Eph. 6:13; 1 Jn. 4:17).

Out of Egypt, THROUGH the wilderness, into the land. God brought Israel out of Egypt by the hand of Moses. Moses was a SHEPHERD. After Moses died, the governmental responsibilities were turned over to Joshua. Joshua was a SOLDIER. Both Moses and Joshua are types of our Lord and Saviour, JESUS CHRIST. Moses himself declared that a Prophet would be raised up like unto him and that Prophet was Jesus (Deut. 18:18; Acts 3:22-23). The names JOSHUA and JESUS mean the same thing: "Jehovah the Saviour." Joshua is a type of Jesus as the Captain of our salvation (Heb. 2:10). Jesus is the General and the HEAD of this army!

The church is on the threshhold of a great harvest. I know that God is moving in an unprecedented fashion, but I prophesy that the decade of the 1980's is the decade of harvest, and growth, and increase for God's people! Glory! All of creation is standing on tiptoe in expectancy of God's outpouring.

Start praying for your city and the pastors of your local area. Give yourself to the Lord Jesus and His Word. Be teachable. Be of one mind and one judgment (1 Cor. 1:10). Learn these principles of the Kingdom and grow up into Christ. You will pay a price. You are on the threshhold of the land. Moses my servant is dead. Now therefore arise!

We have been brought to the edges of His ways. The

land is before us. A new age beckons. Our Heavenly
Joshua is leading us on.

> *"And it came to pass after three days, that the
> officers went through the host* . . . *saying, 'When ye
> see the ARK of the covenant of the Lord your God,
> and the priests the Levites bearing it, then ye shall
> remove from your place, and go after it. Yet there
> shall be a space between you and it, about TWO
> THOUSAND cubits by measure: come not near
> unto it, that ye may know the way by which ye must
> go: for ye have not passed this way heretofore.' And
> Joshua said unto the people, 'Sanctify yourselves:
> for tomorrow the Lord will do wonders among
> you.'* . . . *And as they that bare the ARK were come
> unto Jordan, and the feet of the priests that bare the
> ARK were dipped in the brim of the water, (for
> Jordan overfloweth all his banks all the time of
> harvest,) that the waters which came down from
> above stood and rose up upon an heap very far from
> the city Adam* . . . *" (Josh. 3:2-5,15-16).*

The Ark of the Covenant speaks to us of Jesus Christ
in His KINGSHIP and LORDSHIP. Note that it is
called the Ark of the Covenant "of the Lord of all the
earth" in verse 11. In a time when circumstances say
NO, God is saying to His Church:

> *"Every place that the sole of YOUR foot shall tread
> upon, that have I given unto you* . . . *" (Josh. 1:3).*

It is time to possess the land. Be strong and of a good
courage. The king of Jericho shudders at the thought of
the Overcomer who is within you. Arise and leave the
place of your fear and unbelief, for:

> "It is the time to take the Kingdom,
> Rise up, ye strong, 'tis Christ's command,

For every power and dominion
Is given now into your hand!

Ye that have ears to hear the trumpet,
Ye that have hearts to understand,
It is the time to take the Kingdom,
Rise up, ye strong, possess the land!"

There is a priestly ministry that is upholding His
Lordship. We are walking toward the impossible. But do
not fear, for Jesus the Ark has conquered death and has
opened up the glorious mystery that has been hidden for
generations. Jordan has been divided asunder. The veil
has been rent, and all that was concealed is now made
open to you. The table is spread. Come boldly, for 2000
cubits behind the Ark was a nation that God brought
out so that He might bring them in (Deut. 6:23). Two
thousand years ago, Jesus conquered death, hell, and the
grave, and opened the land of our inheritance. Jordan
was rolled back to ADAM. The Lord Jesus Christ, in His
death and resurrection, cut off every hindrance clear
back to ADAM! He took the keys and he ascended up on
high, leading captivity captive. He arose victorious,
King of kings, and Lord of lords! He has rolled back
every limitation: sin, sickness, poverty, and death (Gal.
3:13). And 2000 years (cubits) later there is a HOLY
NATION, His Glorious Church, that is going to follow
the Ark into the land and walk in everything that He
died for! We are going to put our foot on all enemies. We
are going to reign on the earth (Psa. 2:8; Rev. 5:10)!
We've got a job to do!

You will never conquer Canaan until God has brought
you through the wilderness. Until you learn to press
through tribulation, you will not qualify for God's army.
I am part of this move of God and I want you to be part
of it, too. As I finish this message, there is a sadness in
my heart. Some of you are going to miss out on this
visitation because of those stinking, hellish traditions

that you learned from men. Those lies killed our loved ones and everybody else that learned them (Rom. 8:6) and they will kill us if we don't abandon them in the Name of the Lord (Mk. 7:13). I am not speaking concerning doctrines as much as I am concerning the way that people think . . . the way that we have thought all our lives . . . the lies that have been passed down from generation to generation. And the grand-daddy of all lies is this: "You cannot have anything; you cannot be anything, and you cannot do anything." That stinking lie that says, "You cannot have these things. They are for someone else."

His Body is disjointed. His army lies fragmented (Ezek. 37:1-14); hurting and bruised and wounded. But something is happening! The walls are coming down. The cry and travail of broken humanity and the nagging, haunting travail of a groaning creation is causing us to forget our petty differences. The army that is standing is an army of overcomers. Jesus is their Lord. He has developed them, and they have pressed through their adversities. And on the other side of the wilderness, each of them shall say, "The Spirit of the Lord is upon me!"

AM I CLAY OR AM I GOLD?

"On that foundation anyone may build gold, silver, precious stones, wood, hay, or straw, but in every case the NATURE of his work will come out; the Day will show what it is, for the Day breaks in FIRE, and the FIRE will test the work of each, no matter what that work may be. If the structure raised by any man survives, he will be rewarded; if a man's work is burnt up, he will be a loser—and though he will be saved himself, he will be snatched from the very flames" (1 Cor. 3:12-15—Moffatt).

This is the Day of the Lord. The fire of His Word is

burning in this Day. He is trying everything by that fire, and shaking everything that can be shaken. Only His Kingdom will remain (Heb. 12:26-29). Only that which can stand the test of His Word will survive.

The same hot fire will HARDEN the clay, but it will MELT the gold so that it will flow. The fire is the WORD (Jer. 23:29; Jn. 1:1; Heb. 12:29). The clay is the OLD NATURE (Job 4:17-21; 13:12; Psa. 40:2; Dan. 2:33-44; Hab. 2:6). The gold is the NEW NATURE (Gen. 2:10-11; Job 23:10; Psa. 45:13; Prov. 17:3; 27;21; Mal. 3:3; Rev. 3:14-22). Are you hardening, or are you melting and flowing in worship?

The Word of the Lord in the Day of the Lord is revealing the NATURE of each one of us. The purpose of the fire is to reveal what we are.

Are we clay or are we gold?

"And they overcame him by the blood of the Lamb, and by the word of their testimony; and they loved not their lives unto the death" (Rev. 12:11).

Books and Tapes
By Kelley Varner

How to Order

Your offering for the books and tapes will be used to purchase supplies, purchase and maintain equipment, and, most importantly, to send literature and tapes to ministries and saints in other nations for whom nothing has been prepared (Neh. 8:10).

TAPE CATALOG
To receive a full listing of Kelley's books and tapes, write or call for our current catalog:

Praise Tabernacle
P.O. Box 785
Richlands, N.C. 28574-0785
(919) 324-5026 or 324-5027

PREVAIL: A HANDBOOK FOR THE OVERCOMER— published by Revival Press. Now in its 4th reprinting since 1982. 170 pages. Three major principles: Jesus is Priest and King, Salvation Is Progressive, and Pressing through Tribulation. What is the balance to the "faith" message? What is the transformation of the soul? How are our minds being renewed? Does God want to take us out or bring us through? This book will provide a much-needed balance of the presentation of the foundational truths of the Kingdom of God and will tear down many traditional strongholds. After the Baptism of the Holy Ghost, then what? (16 tapes available)

THE MORE EXECELLENT MINISTRY—published by Destiny Image. 290 pages. We are standing on the threshhold of the Most Holy Place and the fullfillment of the Feast of Tabernacles. There is a Man in the throne who now beckons us to share His Mercy-seat. How does His ministry operate? How do we know that we are called to share this word of reconcilation? Here are new principles for a new day that will enable you to walk successfully during this critical time. There is a new sound in the earth: a sound of reconciliation coming directly from the throne. His previous book, *Prevail*, laid the foundation; *The More Excellent Ministry* begins to build the house. (8 tapes available)

PRINCIPLES OF PRESENT TRUTH FROM GENESIS — 76 pages (4 tapes). What is the Garden of Eden? What is the spiritual significance of Noah's Ark? What are the seven separations of Abraham? What is the Joseph Company? This book is a chapter-by-chapter analysis with an emphasis upon Gen. 1-2 and the life of Abraham. It is the seed-plot of the whole Bible.

PRINCIPLES OF PRESENT TRUTH FROM EXODUS-DEUTERONOMY — 152 pages (4 tapes). What are the three dimensions of the Passover principle? What are five ways to teach the Tabernacle of Moses? What is the significance of the seven Feasts of the Lord? What is the typology of the five major Offerings? Why should every pastor know about the garments of the High Priest? This book places major emphasis upon the Tabernacle of Moses, the Feasts, the Offerings, and the Priesthood. Many diagrams and charts facilitate these studies. Every Bible teacher has to be versed in this.

PRINCIPLES OF PRESENT TRUTH FROM JOSHUA-RUTH — 130 pages (4 tapes). What are principles for possessing the land? What is the Passover of Conquest? What is the significance of the fall of Jericho? Why are the Judges the forerunners of the Kingdom? How can we see in the Book of Ruth a detailed picture of the believer's walk from conception to perfection? This book contains a chapter-by-chapter analysis of Joshua and Judges, and a verse-by-verse study from the Book of Ruth. The entire text of Ruth, using the Hebrew text and other translations, is included. Many charts and diagrams.

PRINCIPLES OF PRESENT TRUTH FROM I-II SAMUEL, I CHRONICLES — 120 pages (4 tapes). Why is there an existing Eli and a growing Samuel? What is the typology of Saul as the old order and David as the new order? What is the panoramic significance of the story of David and Goliath? Why was Jonathan a picture of the man on the fence? What is the Tabernacle of David? This volume highlights Kingdom typology from these O.T. books, emphasizing the lives and the ministries of Samuel, Saul, David and Jonathan. Many charts and diagrams.

PRINCIPLES OF PRESENT TRUTH FROM I-II KINGS, II CHRONICLES — 130 pages (4 tapes). What is the typology of Solomon and his Temple? What is the Elijah ministry? What is the significance of the Sons of the Prophets? This book begins with an in-depth look at Solomon's reign with an emphasis upon the Temple. Each of the subsequent kings of Judah and Israel are analyzed, with an emphasis upon the ministry of the prophets, especially Elijah and Elisha.

PRINCIPLES OF PRESENT TRUTH FROM EZRA-ESTHER — 130 pages (4 tapes). How do these books of restoration parallel the restoration of the Church? What are the twelve gates of Nehemiah? Why does the rebuilding of walls picture the building of the human personality and the transformation of the soul? What is the typology of the Book of Esther and what does it have to do with the day of the Lord? Many charts and diagrams.

PRINCIPLES OF PRESENT TRUTH FROM JOB —118 pages (4 tapes). Pastor Varner considers this volume the most difficult work he has attempted. Why do the righteous suffer? Was God or the devil to blame for Job's plight? Why are Eliphaz, Bildad, and Zophar a picture of the soul of man? Why is Elihu a second-day ministry? Who are Behemoth and Leviathan? Why is Jesus our Heavenly Job? What is the significance of the restoration of Job? This book is a chapter-by-chapter and verse-by-verse study and is a most unique presentation.

PRINCIPLES OF PRESENT TRUTH FROM PSALMS 1-72 — 154 pages (4 tapes). Who wrote the psalms and how are they categorized? What kinds of musical instruments were used in the Bible? What is the importance of Zion and the Tabernacle of David? This book is a chapter-by-chapter and verse-by-verse study of each of these psalms. Outlines and background material is included with each chapter. A must for minstrels.

PRINCIPLES OF PRESENT TRUTH FROM PSALMS 73-150 — 156 pages (4 tapes). Who was Asaph? What is the significance of Psalm 119? What are the Songs of Degrees and how do they picture the believer's ascent into Zion or the ascent of the soul into union with the spirit? This book is a chapter-by-chapter and a verse-by-verse study of each of the remaining Psalms. A must for minstrels.

PRINCIPLES OF PRESENT TRUTH FROM PROVERBS — 118 pages (4 tapes). Why is Proverbs a book about sonship? How can we release the wisdom of God? What is the significance of the Strange Woman and the Virtuous Woman and how do these picture two kinds of minds? This volume includes a thorough introduction and a verse-by-verse study of chapters 1-9 and 30-31. It is great for young people, for chapters 10-29 are presented under 40 topical headings, analyzing areas of practical, daily Christian living.

PRINCIPLES OF PRESENT TRUTH FROM ECCLESIASTES AND THE SONG OF SOLOMON — 142 pages. Why is Ecclesiastes the book of the natural mind? Who is the Preacher? What is life under the sun? How is Ecclesiastes 12 a picture of an order or age that is dying? Who is the Shulamite? What is the relationship between Brideship and Sonship? How is the Song a picture of the development of the believer from conception to perfection? What are seven ways to teach the Song of Solomon? This book gives a thorough introduction to each of these neglected O.T. books. Many fresh insights are opened from Ecclesiastes. The Song is done verse-by-verse! It includes the entire text, other translations, key principles and a continuous story line! (4 tapes on Ecclesiates and 4 tapes on the Song of Solomon)

PRINCIPLES OF PRESENT TRUTH FROM ISAIAH 1-39 — 148 pages (4 tapes). Who was the man Isaiah? What is the Day of the Lord? Who is the Branch? What are the Seven Spirits of God? Who is Lucifer? What is the significance of Zion? This book furnishes a thorough introduction to the whole book of Isaiah. It is presented in a chapter-by-chapter, verse-by-verse format. An overview of all the prophetical books is included.

PRINCIPLES OF PRESENT TRUTH FROM ISAIAH 40-66 — 120 pages (4 tapes). Who is the Servant of Jehovah? Why does the Servant become servants after chapter 53? Who was Cyrus and what is the significant typology pertaining to him? How are Isaiah 58-66 an overview of the Feast of Tabernacles? What is the nation born in a day? This book furnishes a chapter-by-chapter and verse-by-verse study of the remaining chapters of Isaiah. A separate 20-tape series on a verse-by-verse study of Isaiah 53 also.

PRINCIPLES OF PRESENT TRUTH FROM JEREMIAH — 156 pages (8 tapes). Who was the man Jeremiah? How is he a prophet to the nations? How does this important book supplement the history of Kings and Chronicles? Who is the modern-day "Judah" to whom this message is sent? What is the significance of the potter's wheel? What about false pastors and shepherds? What is the meaning of each message to the various nations? What about the fall of Babylon? This book furnishes a chapter-by-chapter and verse-by-verse study of this important prophecy.

PRINCIPLES OF PRESENT TRUTH FROM EZEKIEL — 138 pages (8 tapes). This volume was co-authored with Bill Britton's notes. Why is Ezekiel an end-time book? What did Ezekiel see in chapter one? What is the glory of the Lord? What is the eschatological significance of chapters eight and nine? What are the cherubim? How do Ezekiel's prophecies to the nations compare with those of

Isaiah and Jeremiah? How does the prophet deal with false ministries in chapter 34? What about the New Covenant of chapter 36? What is the meaning of the vision of the dry bones? Who are Gog and Magog? What temple did Ezekiel see in chapters 40-48? How does this book compare to the Book of Revelation? This volume is a chapter-by-chapter and verse-by-verse treatment of the entire text of this neglected prophecy.

THE TABERNACLE OF MOSES — 100 pages (8 or 24 tapes). What are five ways to teach this pattern of heavenly things? Whose mansion is it? What is the significance of the Ark of the Covenant and the Most Holy Place? This book is filled with notes and outlines. This revelation must be mastered to fully understand the Word of God. Many drawings, charts, and outlines. A must for Bible teachers.

THE SERMON ON THE MOUNT — 50 pages (from 8 to 40 tapes). What is the Kingdom of God? How many kingdoms are there? What is the motive and the purpose of the Kingdom? Why is the Church the instrument of the Kingdom? This is an in-depth study of the Kingdom of God. It is a verse-by-verse study of Matthew 5-7, emphasizing the Beatitudes (the Preamble) and the principles (laws) of Christian living. This material will help a new believer and also challenge the more serious Bible student. Very practical. For those who want to know the purpose of the baptism of the Holy Ghost.

THE TONGUE OF THE LEARNED — with J. L. Dutton — over 60 pages (56 tapes to date). What is the preeminence of the Lord Jesus Christ? What does the Bible say about the Kingdom of God? How do we walk with the Lord? What does Scripture say about the Father-son relationship? What about the ministry of the Holy Spirit? Are the gifts of the Holy Spirit (a study of spiritual ministry) for us today? What are the Bible principles governing prayer, praise, and worship? What is the importance of the Church? What is the role and purpose of the Local Church? This book gives the definitions of 335 Bible terms under nine practical headings. It teaches the vocabulary of the Kingdom studied from the original languages of the Bible. Excellent for the classroom. Used in many Bible schools and churches, both here and abroad. If you have just been introduced to the Kingdom message, this volume is what you need.

CHOOSE YE THIS DAY: THE CONFLICTS OF JONATHAN — 34 pages (8 tapes). Why is Saul a picture of the old order? Why is Jonathan a hypocrite? What is the significance of the battle between David and Goliath? Is the Church the Seed of David? What does Saul's encounter with the witch of Endor have to do with the rise of the occult today? This book is in sermon form and tells of the life and ministry of the son of King Saul. A study of the old order and the new order from I Samuel 13-31. For the man on the fence.

THE HOLY GHOST BAPTISM — 35 pages (16 tapes). Who is the Holy Spirit? What is His ministry in the Old and New Testaments? Is the Holy Ghost Baptism a present reality for the Church? What are three New Testament purposes for speaking with tongues? How to minister and receive this experience. Excuses are answered with Scriptures. More answers are given to the most frequently asked questions. Bible terminology. Every pastor needs this book.

THE LAND AND THE THRONE — 44 pages (4 tapes). What is the significance of Jesus' being the Seed of Abraham and the Seed of David? What is the inheritance of the believer? Is it a mansion of gold or the multitude of the nations? This book is an in-depth study of the Abrahamic and Davidic Covenants. Jesus has the land and Jesus has the Throne. The Land is the Earth, and the Throne is the right to rule it! A return to Covenant Theology. Keys to eschatology.

THE HOUR IS COME — 28 pages (4 tapes). What is the glorification of the Son of man? Who is the corn of wheat? Why do we want to go to hell? How low will you go? This book in sermon form is an exegesis of John 12:20-33. A real challenge to world evangelism. The time is now!

THE TWELVE GATES OF THE CITY — 27 pages (16 tapes). Is the city of Revelation 21 a literal city? What is the Bible truth about Heaven? What about the mansions and the golden streets? The gates of pearl? How does the Christ nature progressively unfold from within the believer? How does the city come from heaven to earth, from the invisible to the visible realm? This book of notes is a verse-by-verse study of Revelation 21. The old order concept of Heaven is examined. The city is a people. A study of Genesis 49 and the sons of Jacob — from Reuben to Benjamin. For teachers.

THE POWER OF THE FLAMING SWORD — 21 pages (8 tapes). What is the flaming sword? How powerful are the words which we speak? What does the Bible have to say about the sword? This book in sermon form is a message concerning our speaking the creative Word of the Lord. This is emphasized in the areas of prayer, praise, and prophecy.

THE IMPORTANCE OF THE HOME AND FAMILY— 30 pages (1 tape). What is the importance of the home as the basic unit of society? What is the parallel between the home and the Local Church? What are the two institutions that God has ordained and what is the order of authority in each? What is the significance of the home being a wineskin? What connection is there between the Elijah ministry and the home? This book in sermon form is the first of 12.

A LAMB FOR A HOUSE — 39 pages (1 tape). What is God's method of bringing a nation out of bondage? What is the Passover of the Kingdom? What are the characteristics of the lamb? What about spiritual immunity? This book in sermon form is an exegesis of Exodus 12 and is an excellent study about the home and family. Good for pastors and teachers.

KINGDOM PRINCIPLES FOR THE HOME — 43 pages (1 tape). What is the principle of love? What is the principle of mutual respect? What is the principle of open communication? This book in sermon form gives a unique study of the Bible definition of love from the New Testament Greek of I Corinthians 13:1-13 (plus the use of several other translations).

SKYWALKERS — 44 pages (8 tapes). What examples for teenagers are provided in Samuel, David, Esther, Ruth, Joash, Jesus and others? How can our young people live in the heavenlies today? This study was prepared by Pastor Varner for our teens. He was assisted by Sue Baird. Other local churches are now using this series to teach their young people. This very practical class was taught as part of the curriculum of our Christian school.

DARE TO BE DIFFERENT — 30 pages (8 tapes). Another good book for teens, this was presented in our Christian school. There are two kingdoms. We must dare to be different in our attitude, obedience, joy, meditation, dependability, gratefulness, discernment, perception, enthusiasm, kindness, forgiveness, modesty and boldness. These are characteristics of young people who are walking in the Kingdom of God. These 13 lessons are also excellent Sunday school material.

FOUR FOUNDATIONS OF EFFECTUAL PRAYER— 24 pages (8 tapes). There is a tremendous emphasis on prayer at this time. Here is examined a familiar subject from a fresh perspective. We need to understand prayer from God's side of the Covenant. His thanksgiving for us, His righteousness to us, His boldness through us, and

His compassion among us are four principles which must be understood.

A VISION OF YOUR WORTH — 28 pages (4 tapes). Every Christian must know His worth in Christ. Worthy is the Lamb! What is the worthy portion? What does it mean to be counted worthy? Who is the lambkin? The answers to these questions will help the believer to become all he can in the Lord.

SING, O BARREN — 28 pages (4 tapes). God wants every one of us to be fruitful. We can see keys to this by studying the lives of Sarah, Rebekah, Rachel, Manoah's wife, Hannah, Elizabeth and Mary. We must travail so that the Christ within us can be formed. There are seven powerful truths coming forth from the Body of Christ.

THE RAPTURE — 40 pages (12 tapes). An up-to-date look at Daniel's prophecy of Seventy Weeks and a fresh re-examination of contemporary eschatology.

PRAISE TABERNACLE CORRESPONDENCE COURSE

UNDERSTANDING THE KING AND HIS KINGDOM — A one-, two-, or three-year study program — "36 Steps Toward Your Understanding the Bible." Certificates will be given for the completion of each of the first two years and a diploma for the completion of the third year. Write today for your free brochure.

Additional Available Tape Series

Jesus, Lord of the Home (12 tapes)
Are You Ready for the Third Dimension? (8 tapes)
Israel: God's Chosen People (8 tapes)
The Kingdom of God (8 tapes)
Spiritual Ministry (12 tapes)
Servant Power (8 tapes)
Four-fold Definition of the Local Church (16 tapes)

The New Testament Local Church (32 tapes)
Halloween, Christmas, Easter (8 tapes)
God's Two Greatest Mysteries (8 tapes)
The Coming of the Lord (12 tapes)
Women's Ministry (8 tapes)
The Book of Acts (8 tapes)
Principles of Kingdom Finance (8 tapes)
Bible Patterns of the Kingdom (12 tapes)
The Faith of God (8 tapes)
The Five-fold Ministry (12 tapes)
Life and Immortality (12 tapes)
Water Baptism (8 tapes)
The Day of Atonement (8 tapes)
Principles of Restoration (12 tapes)
The Will of God (8 tapes)
The Songs of Degrees (16 tapes)
The Emerging Christ (12 tapes)
Apostolic Principles (12 tapes)
Romans, Verse-by-verse (from 8 to 30 tapes)
The Feast of Tabernacles (16 tapes)
The More Excellent Ministry (8 tapes) — these are the
    original tapes preached at the House of Prayer in 1981

TAPE OF THE MONTH
Each month two cassette tapes are made available by
Pastor Varner. These messages are ministered by him
and others in the five-fold ministry. You may join this
growing list of listeners on a monthly offering basis.

VIDEO CASSETTES
We are just beginning this new avenue of ministry.
Presently available are three two-hour video cassettes on

the Book of Ruth. This teaching is a verse-by-verse exegesis concerning the Christian walk from conception to perfection, from birth to maturity. Please write or call for more information.

SEMINARS AND CONVENTIONS
There are annual meetings here in Richlands for the Body of Christ. Please inquire for information on the next meeting. There is a team of ministry here at Praise Tabernacle that is available to your local church to teach the principles of restoration and assist in the areas of praise and worship. Please contact Pastor Varner.